MICHAEL JACKSON

KING OF POP
1958 – 2009

EMILY HERBERT

MICHAEL JACKSON
KING OF POP
1958 – 2009

JOHN BLAKE

Published by John Blake Publishing Ltd,
3 Bramber Court, 2 Bramber Road,
London W14 9PB, England

www.johnblakepublishing.co.uk

First published in paperback in 2009

ISBN: 978 1 84454 897 2

British Library Cataloguing-in-Publication Data:

A catalogue record for this book is available from the British Library.

Design by www.envydesign.co.uk

Printed in Great Britain by CPI Bookmarque, Croydon, CR0 4TD

1 3 5 7 9 10 8 6 4 2

Papers used by John Blake Publishing are natural, recyclable products
made from wood grown in sustainable forests. The manufacturing processes
conform to the environmental regulations of the country of origin.

THE STARS PAY TRIBUTE TO THE KING OF POP

'I can't stop crying over the sad news. I have always admired Michael Jackson. The world has lost one of the greats, but his music will live on forever. My heart goes out to his three children and other members of his family. God bless.'

MADONNA

'I am so very sad and confused with every emotion possible... I am heartbroken for his children, who I know were everything to him and for his family. This is such a massive loss on so many levels. Words fail me.'

LISA MARIE PRESLEY

'The last time we saw him he was in London a few weeks ago... He was absolutely fine. I can't believe this, it's such a shock.'

MARK LESTER (CHILD ACTOR AND
GODFATHER TO JACKSON'S CHILDREN)

'He was my idol, he was a role model, he was someone to cry to when my childhood was unbearable, he was a brother; he was a dear friend.'

COREY FELDMAN, EIGHTIES FILM STAR
(WRITTEN ON HIS WEBSITE)

'I'm shocked and devastated. I am hoping this is a dream I will wake up from, but it is not. Michael is dead. For him not to be around, that he's gone, is just surreal. It cannot sink into my psyche. He was a genius.'

URI GELLER

'I think we'll mourn his loss, as well as the loss of ourselves as children listening to *Thriller* on the record player. Dazed in the studio. A major strand of our cultural DNA has left us. RIP, MJ.'

JOHN MAYER

'Michael Jackson was my inspiration. Love and blessings.'

MILEY CYRUS

'Sending my love and prayers out to Michael and his family.'

LINDSAY LOHAN

'Wow! I am truly in shock that Michael Jackson has passed away! I love you, Jackson family. My prayers are with the whole family.'

KIM KARDASHIAN

'The world has suffered a great loss today in Michael Jackson. My thoughts and prayers are with his family, friends, and fans. God bless, God rest his soul, he will live on forever. Life is so short, enjoy every second God gives you.'

HEIDI MONTAG

'A wonderful man and will be greatly missed.'

BRITNEY SPEARS

'Michael Jackson showed me that you can actually see the beat. He made the music come to life. He made me believe in magic. I will miss him.'

P. DIDDY

'When we worked together on *Bad*, I was in awe of his absolute mastery of movement on the one hand, and of the music on the other... Every step he took was absolutely precise and fluid at the same time. It was like watching quicksilver in motion. He was wonderful to work with, an absolute professional at all times, and – it really goes without saying – a true artist. It will be a while before I can get used to the idea that he's no longer with us.'

MARTIN SCORSESE

'Just as there will never be another Fred Astaire or Chuck Berry, or Elvis Presley, there will never be anyone comparable to Michael Jackson... His talent, his wonderment and his mystery make him legend.'

STEVEN SPIELBERG

'[I'm] having a million different reactions I didn't expect I would feel... He was a great singer – God gives you certain gifts, and this child was just an extraordinary child touched by this ability. He could sing like nobody else and he was able to connect with people.'

CHER

'I am overwhelmed by this tragedy. Michael Jackson has been an idol for me all my life. He was not only a talented person but he was unique – a genius. It's such a loss. It feels like when Kennedy died, when Elvis died. My sympathy goes to the family. It's a big loss and it's not even sinking in right now.'

CELINE DION

'I will be mourning my friend, brother, mentor and inspiration... He gave me and my family hope. I would never have been me without him.'

MC HAMMER

'We have lost a genius and a true ambassador of not only pop music, but of all music. He has been an inspiration to multiple generations, and I will always cherish the moments I shared with him onstage and all of the things I learned about music from him and the time we spent together. My heart goes out to his family and loved ones.'

JUSTIN TIMBERLAKE

'He was magic; he was what we all strive to be. He will always be the King of Pop.'

BEYONCÉ

'I am stunned. My friend Michael Jackson is dead.'
JANE FONDA

'Rarely has the world received a gift with the magnitude of artistry, talent and vision as Michael Jackson. He was a true musical icon whose identifiable voice, innovative dance moves, stunning musical versatility and sheer star power carried him from childhood to worldwide acclaim. A 13-time Grammy recipient, Michael's career transcends musical and cultural genres, and his contributions will always keep him in our hearts and memories.'
NEIL PORTNOW, PRESIDENT, NATIONAL ACADEMY RECORDING ARTS & SCIENCES (NARAS)

'My heart is overcome with sadness for the devastating loss of my true friend Michael. He was an extraordinary friend, artist and contributor to the world. I join his family and his fans in celebrating his incredible life and mourning his untimely passing.'
BROOKE SHIELDS

'He was a kind, genuine and wonderful man. He was also one of the greatest entertainers that ever lived. I loved him very much and I will miss him every remaining day of my life.'
LIZA MINNELLI

'Michael Jackson was easily as influential as James Brown, and that's saying a lot. He was the Fred Astaire of his time.'

ALICE COOPER

'He lives forever in my heart. I will never forget the day he came to see me in the studio and I played him music... R I P to Michael Jackson, my music god... Some lost Elvis Presley and we lost Michael Jackson... I cried today because Michael Jackson was a father that we all lost!'

WYCLEF JEAN

'Michael, you left such a legacy on this earth, have touched so many. We thank you for such a driving inspiration in music and our lives. This has got to be one of the saddest days in music history. Michael, Rest In Peace. We miss you.'

KELLY ROWLAND

'My heart... my mind... are broken. I loved Michael with all my soul and I can't imagine life without him. We had so much in common and we had such loving fun together. I was packing up my clothes to go to London for his opening when I heard the news. I still can't believe it; I don't want to believe it. It can't be so. He will live in my heart forever, but it's not enough.

My life feels so empty. I don't think anyone knew how much we loved each other. The purest, most giving love I've ever known. Oh God! I'm going to miss him. I can't yet imagine life without him. But I guess with God's help... I'll learn. I keep looking at the photo he gave me of himself, which says, "To my true love Elizabeth, I love you forever." And I will love him forever.'

DAME ELIZABETH TAYLOR

'I am absolutely devastated at this tragic and unexpected news. For Michael to be taken away from us so suddenly at such a young age, I just don't have the words. Divinity brought our souls together on *The Wiz* and allowed us to do what we were able to throughout the 80s. To this day, the music we created together on *Off The Wall*, *Thriller* and *Bad* is played in every corner of the world and the reason for that is because he had it all... talent, grace, professionalism and dedication. He was the consummate entertainer and his contributions and legacy will be felt upon the world forever. I've lost my little brother today, and part of my soul has gone with him.'

QUINCY JONES

'I am shocked beyond words. It's like a dream – a bad dream. This cannot be! How can Michael Jackson not be here? As a kid, Michael was always beyond his years. He had a knowingness about him that was incredible. When I first heard him sing Smokey's song, "Who's Lovin' You" at 10 years old, it felt like he had lived the song for 50 years.

'Somehow, even at that first meeting with him, he had a hunger to learn, a hunger to be the best, and was willing to work as hard and as long as it took. I had no concern about his ability to go to the top. He was like my son. He had warmth, sensitivity and two personalities. When he was not on stage, he was loving, respectful and shy. When he was on stage, he was so in charge you would not believe he was the same person.

'Michael was, and will remain one of the greatest entertainers that ever lived. He was exceptional, artistic and original. He gave the world his heart and soul through his music. I extend my sympathies to Joe, Katherine and the entire Jackson family. My prayers are with them.'

BERRY GORDY

'It is always hard to lose a friend. I will miss Michael and all that he brought to the world through his music and his creative genius. I know his legend will live on and the world will miss him dearly.'

SMOKEY ROBINSON

'Words cannot begin to express my heartfelt sorrow upon hearing the news of Michael Jackson's passing. I was blessed to be able to work with, and witness first hand, his tremendous talent and growth through the years as he truly became an icon. Today we have all lost a legend, who has touched each of our lives through his music and showmanship over the past five decades. To his family, the entire Jackson clan, and to all his adoring legions of fans throughout the world, my prayers and deepest condolences to all.'

PAULA ABDUL

'Michael Jackson will live forever through the thing that he put all of his life energy into: his music. I will do my part to keep the melody alive, to keep the energy forever changing form, but never, ever dying. Long live Michael Jackson.'

NE-YO

'Words can't begin to describe my sadness for the loss of Michael Jackson. I was honored and humbled to have the opportunity to perform with him several times and he had a profound influence on my career. Michael forever changed the world of music and entertainment, and I will always remember him for his kind and sweet spirit.'

JC CHASEZ

'You cannot say enough about what he has given to us, musically and culturally. We take for granted people like him... all he wanted to do was give us great music and that's what he did. Every single day was dedicated to us. I'll tell you this: seeing him in concert in 1983, the Victory concert with his brothers, to watch people faint in the audience. Grown men fainting, women fainting just because he was that dynamic... all you can say is that you hope we put our arms around his family. So much turmoil toward the end of his career... and I think that's the only thing that you can really hope for is that there is finally peace to this whole situation.'

JAMIE FOXX

'I was lucky enough to know and work with Michael Jackson in his prime. Michael was an extraordinary talent and a truly great international star. He had a troubled and complicated life and despite his gifts, remains a tragic figure. My wife Deborah and I will always have great affection for him.'

JOHN LANDIS

'Michael Jackson, the consummate artist and creative entertainer whom I have known since he was a teenager, is dead. How difficult it is to construct that sentence. We are out of our joy and he is out of his pain. Several generations have not lived a day without Michael Jackson in their lives. I remember his performance, along with the Jackson 5, at the first Black Expo. I remember Suzanne de Passe taking the boys, as their chaperone, to Fred Segal to buy clothes. I observed him from the Regal Theater to Expo, to "We Are The World" to "Thriller", to "Beat It" – he was always there.'

REV. JESSE JACKSON

'I am shocked and saddened by Michael's passing. I, along with his millions of fans, looked forward to seeing him tour one more time. Now may he rest in peace.'

TINA TURNER

'Michael Jackson is the reason why I do music and why I am an entertainer. I am devastated by this great loss, and I will continue to be humbled and inspired by his legacy. My prayers are with his family. Michael will be deeply missed, but never forgotten. He's the greatest... the best ever. No one will ever be better.'

CHRIS BROWN

'I grew up with Michael Jackson. He was a good friend and the most exciting and innovative entertainer to have lived.'

NAOMI CAMPBELL

CONTENTS

1   DEATH OF A SUPERSTAR   1

2   A STAR IS BORN   23

3   CHILD PRODIGY ON THE LOOSE   43

4   MICHAEL JACKSON – SUPERSTAR   65

5   THE GREATEST ALBUM EVER MADE   87

6   DISASTER STRIKES   115

7   FINDING NEVERLAND   137

8   THE MOONWALKER   159

9   SCANDAL   183

10   A MARRIAGE OF DYNASTIES   203

11   A FAMILY MAN   219

12   THE FINAL YEARS   239

About the Author

Emily Herbert is a highly successful journalist and author. Having written for a host of newspapers and magazines, she has a unique insight into the lives of the stars and the inner circle of celebrities. Her previous books include: *Gok Wan – The Biography*; *Katie and Peter – Too Much in Love*; *Kerry – Story of a Survivor* and *Arise Sir Terry Wogan*

CHAPTER ONE

DEATH OF A SUPERSTAR

The scene was pandemonium. Paramedics from the Los Angeles Fire Department swarmed around the large, rented home in Holmby Hills, LA, desperate to revive the prone figure in their midst. They pumped his chest in an attempt to get a response, but all in vain. Meanwhile, the entourage surrounding him was hysterical, screaming, 'You've got to save him, you've got to!' Eventually, he was transported to an ambulance, where attempts to resuscitate him continued, and rushed to University of California at Los Angeles Hospital, a six-minute drive away, where doctors worked frantically to get a pulse. But it was no good. Michael Jackson died, aged 50, on 25 June 2009, after suffering a massive heart attack at his home. One of the greatest geniuses in pop-music history was gone.

As news of his death began to spread, stunned members of the public gathered outside. More than 10 members of Michael's entourage had followed the ambulance in two BMW 4x4s, including his brother, Randy, who had also been with him when he collapsed. His sister, La Toya, was seen running into the hospital in tears. Katherine, Michael's much beloved mother, made her way from the family compound in Encino, just north of LA, to see her son's body.

Los Angeles County coroner Fred Corall confirmed the devastating news. 'We were notified by the West Los Angeles Police detectives that Mr Jackson was transported by medics to the hospital,' he said. 'Upon admittance he was unresponsive and was pronounced dead at 2.26pm.'

Right from the start, there was speculation. Michael was less than three weeks away from beginning a massive 50-date concert schedule at London's O2 Arena, titled, 'This Is It'. While this was seen as a comeback and a potential solution to his much-publicised money concerns, there had also been severe doubt that he could cope. By that stage, he had not performed in a major concert for 12 years and with the best will in the world, and there was plenty of it, even his most loyal fans must have been wondering how he would be able to handle such demanding physical and emotional work. And yet the expectation was incredible: the 750,000 tickets for the shows sold out within hours of going on sale. His public wanted to see the return of the King of Pop, as much as the King himself did.

Was the pressure all too much? Was Michael pushing himself too hard, pressurising himself too much and becoming increasingly terrified that his performances could not live up to the glory days? Then there was his addiction to prescription drugs. It had been known for some time that Michael had been wedded to prescription drugs for decades, ever since he suffered horrific injuries filming a commercial for Pepsi, back in 1984. Almost immediately, reports began to surface that shortly before he collapsed, he had been injected with Demerol, a drug similar to morphine.

'Shortly after taking the Demerol, he started to experience slow, shallow breathing,' revealed a source, present at the time. 'His breathing gradually got slower and slower until it stopped; his staff started mouth-to-mouth and an ambulance was called, which got there in eight minutes.'

Across the world, shocked associates were responding to what they had heard. 'I must hear it from a doctor,' said Michael's friend Uri Geller to one reporter. 'I cannot believe everything I see and read and hear at the moment. I hope it's not true, I'm waiting like you are, like the whole planet is waiting, to hear it from the mouth of the doctor taking care of him. I'm absolutely devastated and shocked. He was a young man, terribly fit and basically in good shape.'

As the news sank in, impromptu shrines to Michael Jackson sprang up all over the world. Mourners laid tributes at the foot of the Eiffel Tower, the Hollywood Walk of Fame (which was inundated with them) and city centres in Denmark, Sweden and Russia. Grieving fans lit candles in Prague's Old Town Square and placed flowers outside London's Lyric Theatre, where 'Thriller – Live' was playing. Above all, of course, the Jackson family compound in Hayvenhurst Avenue, Encino, LA, became the focal point for displays of grief: 'India will never forget you,' said one message. There were similar sentiments from Sri Lanka, Mexico, Grenada and Canada. Meanwhile, the news very nearly brought the Internet to a standstill: so many people googled Michael Jackson in the hours after his death that the search engine thought it was under attack and displayed an automated virus alert screen.

As preparations for a funeral and memorial service began, and hundreds of thousands of fans began to descend on Los Angeles, a myriad of details started to emerge about the final years of Michael's life. Although his own financial affairs were in a mess, it was thought that he had left 200 previously unpublished songs, worth a good £60 million, to his children: Prince Michael, 12, Paris Katherine, 11, and Prince Michael II (also known as 'Blanket'), 7. Michael's own father Joe paid tribute to his son: 'Michael was the biggest superstar in the world and in history,' he said, and for once the superlatives were spot-on. 'He was loved by everybody, whether poor or wealthy or whatever may be.' The children, meanwhile, were in the care of Michael's mother Katherine, although their birth mother, Debbie Rowe, Michael's second wife, also expressed an interest in looking after them.

In the days that followed, emergency chiefs released a transcript of the call staff made to try and revive Michael. Apart from anything else, such was the level of his fame and the shock surrounding his death that everyone involved wanted to make it clear from the start that there had been no foul play, that they had worked as hard as they could to revive him. The transcript read as follows:

A (ambulance man): 'What is the nature of your emergency?'

B (member of Jackson's staff): 'I need an ambulance as soon as possible, sir.'

A: 'OK, sir, what's your address?'

B: 'It's 100 North Carolwood Drive, Los Angeles, California, 90007.'

A: 'OK, sir, and what's the phone number you are calling from?'

B: 'xxxxxx [number has been erased from transcript].'

A: 'OK, can you tell me what happened?'

B: 'Well, sir, we have a gentleman here and he needs help, and he's not breathing and we're trying to pump him, but he's not responding.'

A: 'OK, OK, how old is he?'

B: 'He's 50 years old, sir.'

A: 'OK, OK. He's not conscious? He's not breathing?'

B: 'Yes, he's not breathing, sir.'

A: 'He's not conscious, either?'

B: 'No, he's not conscious, sir.'

A: 'All right, is he on the floor?' Where is he at right now?'

B: 'He's on the bed, sir.'

A: 'OK, let's get him down onto the floor. I'm gonna help you with CPR right now.'

B: 'We need him – we need?...'

A: 'We're already on our way there. We're already on our way there. I'm doing all I can to help you over the phone. We're on our way. Did anybody see him?'

B: 'Sir, we have a personal doctor here with him, sir.'

A: 'Oh, you have a doctor there?'

B: 'Yeah, but he's not responding to anything – no, no medicine – he's not responding to anything – to CPR or anything.'

A: 'Oh. OK. Well, we're on our way there. If your guy's doing CPR and you're being instructed by a doctor there on the scene, then he has a higher authority than me. Did anybody witness what happened?'

B: 'Er, no, it's just the doctor, sir. The doctor's been the only one here.'

A: 'OK, so did the doctor see what happened?'

B: 'Doctor, did you see what happened?' (Mumbled voice of panicked doctor can be heard saying, 'Tell them, they need to come!')

B: 'Sir, um, you just, you need to come, please.'

A: 'We're on our way. I'm just passing these questions on to our paramedics, but they are on their way there, sir.'

B: 'Thank you. He's pumping… he's pumping his chest, but he's not responding, sir. Come, please.'

A: 'OK. OK, we're on our way. We're less than a mile away and we'll be there shortly.'

B: 'Thank you, sir, thank you.'

A: 'OK, sir. Call us back if you need anything else.'

There was some disquiet that Michael had been on a bed: when CPR is administered, the patient should be on the floor. And the Jackson family was keen to establish exactly what happened. They had known that Michael had been taking Demerol for years, but believed he might have stepped up his intake in recent months to help him cope with the pressure of the O2 concerts.

'This is a case of abuse of medications,' said the

Jacksons' former family lawyer Brian Oxman, who had been at the hospital with them when Michael died. 'This is not something which had been unexpected. Because of the medication that Michael was taking, his family had been trying for months and months and months to take care of Michael Jackson. I don't want to jump to conclusions, and I don't want to point fingers, we don't know what Michael Jackson perished from, but what I do fear is that it was the medications. I spoke to family members: I said if this situation arises where Michael perishes because of these medications I will not hold my tongue, I will speak out and I will speak out loud about the overmedication of Michael Jackson. Michael was rehearsing and working extremely hard. I think he was in discomfort because he was working so very hard.'

The broadcaster Paul Gambaccini agreed. 'It [the concerts] seemed to be too much of a demand on the unhealthy body of a 50-year-old,' he said. 'I wonder if perhaps the stress of preparing for those dates was a factor in his collapse. It was wishful thinking that at this stage of his life he could be Michael Jackson again.'

But Michael had never stopped being Michael Jackson, no matter what problems he'd had in later years, as witnessed by the massive outpouring of grief all around him. Tributes continued to flood in from the great and good, as well as his millions of fans. The police, meanwhile, said they wanted to talk to Michael's personal doctor, Dr. Conrad Murray, who was thought to have administered the painkiller.

Those close to the star, however, revealed that for years they had feared something like this would happen. His first wife, Lisa Marie Presley, spoke out about the fact that Michael himself had feared this might be the manner of his passing, and to go on record about their relationship. 'Years ago, Michael and I were having a deep conversation about life in general,' she wrote on the Internet. 'I can't recall the exact subject matter, but he may have been questioning me about the circumstances of my father's death. At some point he paused, he stared at me very intensely and he stated with an almost calm certainty, "I am afraid that I am going to end up like him, the way he did."

'I tried to deter him from the idea, at which point he just shrugged his shoulders and nodded, almost matter of fact, as if to let me know he knew what he knew, and that was that. Fourteen years later, I am sitting here watching on the news an ambulance leaving the driveway of his home, the big gates, the crowds outside the gates, the coverage, the crowds outside the hospital; the cause of death and what may have led up to it and the memory of this conversation hit me, as did the unstoppable tears. A predicted ending by him, by loved ones and by me, but what I didn't predict was how much it was going to hurt when it happened.

'I am going to say now what I have never said before because I want the truth out there for once. Our relationship was not "a sham" as is being reported in the press. It was an unusual relationship, yes, where two unusual people who did not live or know a "normal life" found a connection, perhaps with some suspect timing on his part. Nonetheless, I do believe he loved me as much as he could love anyone and I loved him very much. I wanted to "save him".'

Alas, even Lisa Marie, who had grown up knowing first hand what the consequences of fame like Michael's could bring, failed to do that.

Another person who was determined to set the record straight and focus attention on the real Michael, not the myths and downright lies that swirled around him, was his fellow child star, Mark Lester. Mark had appeared in the title role of *Oliver!* in the 1968 film, so he knew exactly what it was like having to deal with global fame at a very young age. Unlike Michael, however, he had managed to escape the pressures of it by leaving show business and working as an osteopath. Married for the second time, and with four children of his own, he was also godfather to Michael's three.

'My feelings are for those poor children – I love those kids dearly,' he said. 'They are an extended part of my family.

'They adored Michael and he adored them. He was a

11

really good father; he was a relaxed, natural dad. Michael had a very strict moral code – they were not allowed to run riot, but they are extremely bright and intelligent kids. My happiest memories of Michael are when we relaxed as families together watching DVDs or playing music – just being together. We did that many times.

'I was watching TV in a trance, thinking I'd wake up and find out it was not really happening. I was just numb and shocked. I spoke to Michael only last week and he seemed on pretty good form – so confident and positive. He was really excited about doing those O2 concerts in London; it was going to be the platform for him to get back in there. Michael had it tough – he had some really tough things to go through, but his character was strong and he got through those things. But I saw the real Michael, a dedicated father and a really nice man. He was just a very normal guy – quiet, shy, polite and dignified. To think we will never see that beautiful man again is awful. I'm going to miss him lots.'

Indeed, the two families were so close that they had spent the previous Christmas together in the Middle East. Mark's oldest daughter Lucy had very happy memories of that time and paid testimony to the star's generosity. 'In Dubai, Michael gave me a lap-top computer, a camera and Chanel make-up and perfume, plus Trivial Pursuits and stuff – and he gave Barbie dolls and action figures to my brothers and sisters,' she said. 'His Christmas tree was twice as high as the ceiling in our house and in his kids' rooms were piles and piles of presents. They had 10 of everything. It was just incredible – there was even a Toys R Us van parked outside his mansion.

'Then, when we saw him in London recently, he gave us loads more presents, saying they were late Christmas gifts. I've always had a lot of fun whenever I've met him. The first time was in Las Vegas at an MTV awards – my knees were buckling, I was so nervous. But he was just the kindest person – people don't know what he is like. He loved his family so much – and just enjoyed normal things like going to the cinema and listening to music.'

More details were beginning to emerge about the chaotic scenes at the hospital. 'I went to the UCLA and got there just before Randy did,' Jackson family spokesman and attorney Brian Oxman reported. 'And when he came in, a few minutes later, we just saw each other in the emergency room and he started crying. I had my arms around him. We couldn't speak. Jermaine then came in and tears were streaming down his face, and I said "Jermaine" – and he couldn't talk. He just cried and hugged me. Then he went into the other room, and I knew what had happened.' The police, meanwhile, were keen to make it clear that they were not conducting a criminal investigation, as far as Dr. Murray was concerned: their concern was to piece together a proper timeline.

Michael's manager Frank Dileo was also present and it fell to him to break the news to the children. 'His three children were there,' he told Meredith Vieira on the *Today* show, the day after Michael's death. 'They were in a separate room while the doctors worked on Michael. I'm very sad for his children, his mother, his father, his brothers and sisters. It was a very rough day yesterday for everybody. We had to tell the children. I didn't go in alone; I went in with a doctor and a social worker. The nanny was in there and Dr. Murray, Michael's personal physician. It was, as you would think... I can't even begin to tell you the emotion that flowed out of those children. Michael was a very dedicated parent, a single parent, who took that responsibility very seriously. His whole life surrounded around those children [sic] and they around him.'

But he had been in a bad way, no one could deny that. The extent of Michael's dependence on drugs was revealed by Grace Rwaramba, who had been the children's nanny for years, before finally leaving Michael's employ the previous December. Like so many others, she had tried to save him, but to no avail. 'I had to pump his stomach many times,' she revealed. 'He always mixed so much of it. There was one period that it was so bad that I didn't let the children see him... He always ate too little and mixed too much.'

Grace became so concerned that she tried to enlist the help of his mother Katherine and his sister Janet to get Michael back to good health – but he interpreted her actions in the wrong way and dismissed her. 'He didn't want to listen; that was one of the times he let me go,' she said.

Despite Michael's acknowledged frailty, there was still shock from those who had been working with him. He was extremely thin, certainly, but was managing to recapture some of the old magic in rehearsals, so much so that it was bringing back memories of the glory days. There had seemed a real chance that Michael might stage the comeback so many longed to see.

'He was frail, you might say, but when he arrived for rehearsal something really extraordinary seemed to happen,' said Patrick Woodroffe, lighting engineer for the show. 'He came on stage at 9pm, and we all looked at each other and there was something that said that he really had it. Last night, particularly, he came on stage and he was electric. It was like he had been holding back and suddenly he was performing as everyone had remembered him in the past.'

This was borne out by footage released showing Michael performing at the Staples Center in Los Angeles, in rehearsals for the show. He was very thin, but the energy, and of course, the massive talent were still very much in evidence: Michael was seen singing and dancing to the old classics, including 'Beat It', 'Billie Jean' and 'Thriller'.

'He danced as well or better than the 20-year-old dancers we surrounded him with,' said Randy Phillips, of AEG Live, which was promoting the shows. 'He was riveting. I thought this was going to be the greatest live show ever produced. He was so great, I got goose bumps.' Certainly, a spectacle had been planned, using astonishing props, including a huge spider and an illuminated sphere that Michael would send out into the audience, before it came back to settle on his hand, where it exploded. Now there were talks of releasing this material on DVD.

Ed Alonzo was a magician and comedian who had been brought in to work on the show. 'I just thought, "Wow, he still has it,"' he said. 'When he did *Thriller*, I was just in awe. It was a privilege to be able to watch the concert no one will see now. The choreography, all of it... he just looked fantastic. Michael was such a quick learner. He would learn this stuff in seconds. And jump right into it. He looked great and the moves he was doing on stage with the crew were breathtaking. He didn't seem tired, he didn't even take a moment to grab water or take a rest. He went from one number to the next, saying, "Let's do that again."'

Another witness to the performance was Robert Baker, a dance studio boss involved with the show. 'Michael was in great shape, he definitely wasn't your average 50-year-old,' he said. 'Doctors who checked him out for the insurance firms were amazed. One of them even joked that he had the condition of a 20-year-old. Four dancers from my studio were selected for his tour and were in rehearsals with Michael every day. These kids are in their twenties, but they said Michael was unbelievable and could keep up with them easily.'

Meanwhile, Michael's children, still in utter shock, made it known that they wanted to stay with their grandmother: while Debbie Rowe had expressed an interest in looking after them, they simply didn't have the same relationship with her. The family released a statement: 'They said, "We want to stay with Grandma,"' it read. 'They are upset and they miss their daddy, but they are coping with the help of their family.'

The website TMZ, which broke the news of Michael's death, also reported on what looked to be turning into a bitter custody battle. 'The family feel that Katherine and Joe Jackson are the only people who can help the children understand who their father was, help them grieve, and teach them to deal with life in the spotlight. We're also told the kids are healthy but, as expected, they miss their Daddy. They have no relationship with Debbie Rowe.'

Given the furore surrounding Michael's death, the physician hired the lawyer Edward Chernoff to represent him. Chernoff denied the reports that Dr. Murray had injected Michael with Demerol, or indeed any other substances: 'There was no Demerol. No OxyContin. He checked for a pulse. There was a weak pulse in his femoral artery. He started administering CPR. He was the one who suggested the autopsy to the family while they were still in the hospital. He didn't understand why Michael Jackson had died.'

As for the fact that he was on a bed rather than the floor, a spokeswoman said, 'As Jackson is frail and small, and heart pumping can be quite forceful, Murray thought the bed was better.'

Michael's mother, Katherine, was formally awarded temporary guardianship of the children: she put in a petition arguing that they, 'have a long-established relationship with [their] paternal grandmother and are comfortable in her care.' Joe supported the move, but voiced suspicions that all was not as it should have been.

'Michael was dead before he left the house,' he said. 'I'm suspecting foul play somewhere. He was waving to everybody and telling them he loves them and all the fans at the gate. A few minutes after Michael was out there he was dead. Yes, I have a lot of concerns. I can't get into that, but I don't like what happened. My family is doing pretty good, yes they are. It has been really tough. Remember, we have just lost the biggest star in the world, the biggest superstar in the world.'

Details of the will were published: some money was left to charity, but most of the estate was divided between Katherine and the three children. Katherine was also nominated guardian, with the proviso that, if she couldn't look after the children, Michael wanted Diana Ross to do it. That estate, whatever the reality of Michael's finances at the time of his death, was set to be a big one: Elvis Presley had also been in a financial mess at the time of his death, but after his ex-wife Priscilla (Lisa Marie's mother) intervened, successful management turned it into a multi-million pound business.

The same looked set to happen to Neverland. Michael had not lived at the ranch for four years, having left after being acquitted in the sex abuse trial of 2005, but despite the various dramas involving his finances, he still owned it, or at least a chunk of it. It was also the place most closely associated with him, and with careful planning, could end up a lasting monument to him. His former wife Debbie Rowe was not mentioned at all.

In fact, she chose this moment to announce that Michael was not the biological father of the children. But in fairness, did it matter? From the moment they were born, Michael had brought the children up as his own and the bond between them was clear for all to see.

There was a story circulated in the media that Michael might leave his share of the Beatles back catalogue to Paul McCartney in his will, but this did not happen. Reports surfaced that McCartney was mortified at this oversight. As a matter of fact, the story was a complete fabrication and it prompted the former Beatle to post a message on his website stating just that – and that reports of his devastation were of course entirely untrue.

Randy Phillips revealed more about the last days of rehearsals, saying that Michael would eat small amounts of vegetarian lasagne, steamed broccoli, nut loaf or tofu with chilli sauce. 'He used to forget to eat because he was so focused, and Kenny Ortega and I used to cut up his food and physically feed him,' he said. 'Frail, he certainly wasn't. He was always very thin, but not to the point where he couldn't perform. He really kicked into high gear and was totally engaged in the last two weeks. Before that he was nervous and not really coming to rehearsals.

'But that was his schedule and that was how he wanted to do things. It was like when you revise the day before an exam – that was the way he operated. Michael did not have a gruelling schedule, he had *Michael's* schedule. He didn't need to rehearse that much; he was so talented that he didn't need to. When he started dancing, he was dancing better than the best 20-year-old dancers in the world, he was that good.'

They had actually been working together on the day of his death. 'He did a three-hour rehearsal and we all finished up at 12.30am on Thursday morning,' he continued. 'He was really excited. He was super-charged and did a group hug with the director Kenny Ortega and his manager. He was like a kid in the candy store, he was so up for it. I walked him out to the car and he put his arm around me and, speaking softly like he always does, he said to me: "Do you know what? We are here! We are going to make it. I love you for doing this and now I know I can do it!"'

Given the circumstances, it was decided to hold the memorial service at the Staples Center, where Michael had been rehearsing his big comeback. There was speculation that it might be held in Neverland, but the logistics were deemed too difficult, and so 17,500 tickets were to be made available through an online free lottery. However, hundreds of thousands of mourners were expected to make their way to the city, on Tuesday, 7 July 2009, to pay their last respects, and it was now known that quite a send-off was planned. Michael was to lie in state in a gold casket, centre stage once more, where he belonged.

In a break with convention, the memorial service was being held before the funeral, rather than after it: this was because the family was still awaiting the second autopsy report. The Jacksons, meanwhile, would attend a small, private ceremony before the larger, public one to say their own goodbyes.

And so ended one of the most extraordinary careers in show business. Michael Jackson had his problems, no one would gainsay that, but he carved a notch in showbiz history, and in so doing formed a bond with fans that never really faded away. His death, like those of Marilyn Monroe, John F. Kennedy, Elvis and Princess Diana, turned into one of those 'where were you?' moments – no one would ever forget where they were when they heard the news.

The King of Pop was dead, but his legacy lingered on. His records started to race up the charts once again, websites faltered as Internet users downloaded videos of Michael performing, and the sense of grief, worldwide, was palpable. But what was it that made Michael Jackson such an exceptional performer? How did a young boy from the industrial heartlands of the US transform himself into such a major star? His story is the stuff of showbiz legend – and it is one that will endure.

CHAPTER TWO
A STAR IS BORN

The audience sat rapt, its collective gaze fixed towards the stage. It was 25 March 1983, a few hours into a large fundraiser at the Pasadena Civic Auditorium, Los Angeles. Everyone who was anyone was present. Titled 'Motown 25: Yesterday, Today, Forever', the show, taped in front of a large audience, was ostensibly to help fight sickle cell disease. Really, it was an opportunity to prove that the Motown record label was as important as it had ever been.

A few big name acts had recently left Motown, including Michael Jackson, Diana Ross and Marvin Gaye, and so naturally there was some curiosity among the audience, made up of industry bigwigs, star performers, the media and the myriad hangers-on that the music business attracts, as to which stars would appear. In the end, Marvin Gaye did perform, alongside The Miracles, Mary Wells and Martha Reeves, Stevie Wonder, The Supremes, The Temptations, and many more.

And then, to the delight of the audience, out stepped the Jackson 5. Throughout the seventies, the family had been one of the most important acts on the label: groundbreakers, money-spinners, and the jewel in the Motown crown. But that had been some years previously. Motown founder Berry Gordy described them as 'the last big stars to come rolling off my assembly line.'

By the time of the concert, Michael was already an established solo performer in his own right: *Thriller*, the best-selling album of all time, had been released in December 1982, breaking one record after another since it first hit the charts.

Nor was this the first album he'd made on his own: indeed, he had been releasing solo material since he was a child, along with the recordings that he continued to do with his brothers. A major breakthrough had come a few years earlier, in 1979, with the release of *Off The Wall*, the album that established him as an adult singer in his own right. Even so, as far as public perception was concerned, there was still something of the adorable little boy lost that Michael had been when he first achieved massive fame at the age of 11; they still hadn't quite got used to the fact that he was now a mature man.

The original five, Michael, Jackie, Marlon, Jermaine and Tito came out, followed by Randy, the youngest of the Jackson brothers, and performed some of their greatest hits: 'I Want You Back', 'The Love You Save' and 'Say You'll Be There'. It was the usual polished performance, laid on by one of the greatest entertainment groups of their day. That night something was slightly different, though. From the start, Michael had always stood out from his siblings, sheer talent and effervescence marking him out as something quite different, but he had always been very much part of the group.

Now, though, he was beginning to stand aside from the other brothers. He was dressed differently, too. They were all in stage costume, but Michael's was not the same: slightly too-short trousers (so you could see his ankles), sharp white socks, a black glittery jacket, one white glove... it was the basis of the look that he was to have throughout much of the eighties, though still in its developmental stage back then.

And then, something strange happened. The other brothers left the stage, leaving Michael in the spotlight on his own. He bowed to the audience, thanked them for their applause, and then said that he loved the old songs, but the new ones were even better. Everyone was alert: no one knew quite what was about to happen. Suddenly, a Trilby appeared at his feet. Still, no one was any the wiser. And then... he struck a pose.

In the background, the band launched into his current chart hit, 'Billie Jean'. Realising that something truly special was about to take place, the crowd erupted. And off he went, dressed in what was to be his trademark garb, flicking the hat away and launching into one of the sharpest dance routines ever seen on TV. Again, silence descended as the audience drank it all in: the high kicks, the twirls on the spot as he effortlessly hit the high 'C', over and over again. Then finally, the now-infamous moonwalk, the mysterious process by which his feet seemed to step forward, while he was actually gliding backward. The crowd erupted again, as they would do twice more for Michael that night, first when the moonwalk was repeated, and then finally as his performance drew to a close.

That was the night when Michael Jackson danced away from his brothers and into the history books. It was the moment when he went from being a cute child star to perhaps the greatest entertainer the world has ever known. This was a defining moment, not just for his career but for pop music too. And although massive success on a scale never seen before was just around the corner – the video of 'Thriller' had yet to be released – nothing in Michael's life ever quite topped what happened that night. No other entertainer has ever managed to equal it, either. He was truly the King of Pop.

★ ★ ★

It was all a far cry from Michael's birth, 25 years previously, when the only prospects that might seem to await him would have been blue-collar work in the American steel industry, just like his dad. Joseph Jackson was himself a highly musical man, although the only real success that he was to find in the industry came through the son that he helped create – and some would say, help to damage. Joe was born on 26 July 1929, in Arkansas, USA. The eldest in a family of four, born to Samuel Jackson and Crystal Lee King, he was to experience a disruptive childhood after his parents separated when he was just 12 years old.

Joe spent the rest of his childhood with his father in Oakland, California, but moved to East Chicago, Indiana, to be near Crystal, at the age of 18. It was an odd foreshadowing of what would happen to his most famous son: as a child Michael was also dominated by his father and ended up being closer to his mother, although in every other way he had a very different upbringing to Joe.

Joe had a brief early marriage, which was annulled, before wooing and wedding Katherine Screws on 5 November 1949. He enjoyed a short career as a boxer (sport and music were two of the main routes for black Americans to scramble their way out of poverty in the 20th century), but ultimately that came to nothing, too. He then went on to work as a crane operator at the

Gary-based U.S. Steel. In the mid-fifties he took a short break, forming an R&B band, The Falcons, with his brother Luther; it was their lack of success that made him drive his own sons so hard in the years ahead. Eventually he was forced to return to the day job, although he and Luther would often jam together in the evenings after work.

Michael was to be much, much closer to his mother. Katherine was born Kattie B. Screws on 4 May 1930 in Barbour County, Alabama, to Martha Mattie Upshaw and Prince Albert Screws, which is the real reason why Michael named two of his children Prince and not the self-aggrandisement later claimed by many. When Kattie was four, her father changed the family surname to Scruse; he also changed his daughter's name to Katherine Esther Scruse and moved the family to East Chicago, Indiana. Later, Katherine would meet Joe there. Sadly, her childhood was marred when she contracted polio at a very young age. Although a full recovery was made, from then on she walked with a limp.

Despite her physical weakness, Katherine was to prove the lynchpin of the family. She was the absolute rock at its base when fame began to take over and then, in later decades, when it drove a wedge between some of them, and they were exhausted by the stress and pressures that enormous success brings. She provided Michael with complete emotional support and stability; she was the

Fans and family pay tribute to the King of Pop at his memorial service on 7th July 2009.

Above left: Two fans add farewell messages to a giant poster of their idol.

Above right: Michael's three children, Paris Katherine, Prince Michael and Prince Michael II (known as Blanket), whose faces had rarely been seen in public before, brave the cameras to say goodbye to their beloved father.

Below: The Jackson brothers with Michael's gold coffin. They all wore sunglasses and a sequinned glove in honour of Michael.

Above left: Young Michael as a pupil at Montclair Prep School, California, in 1973 and, *right*, his yearbook photo. Although the school had a strict haircut policy, Michael was allowed his afro as it was important for his image.

Below: The Jackson 5 (*l-r*): Marlon, Jackie, Tito, Jermaine and Michael, with nine-year-old Randy Jackson in front.

A family affair. The Jackson children (minus Jermaine) in 1976. *Front*: Janet Jackson. *Centre (l-r)*: Randy, La Toya and Rebbie. *Back (l-r)*: Jackie, Michael, Tito and Marlon.

The brothers doing what they did best. Their mother, Katherine, made many of their early stage costumes.

Motown's singing sensations.

Michael relaxing in the family home with his sister, La Toya.

Above left: Michael's first foray into acting. He spent a lot of time preparing for his role as the Scarecrow in his first feature film, *The Wiz*.

Above right: At the premiere for *The Wiz* with his dad, Joe, and mum, Katherine, in 1970.

Below: Performing at the Hammersmith Odeon in London in 1977.

In 1979, Michael was poised to take the world by storm with his new solo album – *Off the Wall*.

mainstay in a rapidly shifting world. Throughout his life, he was to remain devoted to his mother, naming his daughter after her, and his sons after her own father, speaking often of the love he felt for her and all she had done for him. But it wasn't easy for Katherine. A devout Jehovah's Witness, apart from seeing her children go out on the road for very many months of their childhood, she knew that Joe wasn't a faithful husband and she was forced to suffer a great deal in silence. However, her devotion to her children was palpable: right up to the very end, she was there for Michael.

Michael Joseph Jackson was born on 29 August 1958, the seventh of Joseph Walter and Katherine Esther Scruse's nine children. There is a good deal of confusion as to the pecking order, but the siblings appeared thus: Rebbie was first, followed by Jackie, Tito, Jermaine, La Toya, Marlon, Michael, Randy and Janet. In addition, Joe went on to father one child outside marriage: Joh Vonnie Jackson, the youngest of the lot.

Michael was just four when his father hit on the plan to bring fame and fortune to his family. Having got nowhere with The Falcons, his kids would take to the stage instead. And so the first manifestation of the group came into being, made up of Jackie, Jermaine, Tito and Marlon, initially known simply as The Jacksons. At first, Michael would watch his brothers performing. A year later, at the tender age of five, he began singing and dancing himself, copying not only what his brothers were doing, but also learning from the biggest stars of the day that he studied on TV.

Even then Michael's voice stood out from the crowd, while dance-wise, he was capable of imitating the moves of James Brown. Never slow when it came to spotting earning potential in his children, Joe brought him into the group. Of course, at that stage no one realised that Michael would eventually become the dominant figure, head and shoulders above the rest.

Initially, both Michael and Marlon acted as back-up musicians, playing congas and tambourine. But Michael had started to sing, and what a voice he had. Even when he was very young, it had a unique clarity and purity that made him stand out from the crowd. As time went on, these qualities began to show more and more.

It was when he was just eight that Michael and Jermaine took over lead vocals and the Jackson 5 was born. In the early days, the band was a family enterprise, with both parents involved. Money was tight and so Katherine made her sons' costumes: 'She always made all of our clothes,' Michael told Jesse Jackson on the radio show *Keep Hope Alive* in 2005. 'My mother would sew and stitch everything – everything we wore before we were really making it in Motown.'

Meanwhile, through watching other performers, Michael increasingly learned his trade. Now beyond doubt a child prodigy, as far as singing and dancing skills were concerned, he demonstrated abilities far beyond his age. Years later, in 1993, in a major television interview with Oprah Winfrey, Michael recalled those formative influences. 'I think James Brown is a genius, you know, when he's with the Famous Flames, unbelievable,' he told her.

'I used to watch him on the television, and I used to get angry at the cameraman because whenever he would really start to dance, they would be on a close-up so I couldn't see his feet. I'd shout, "Show him, show him!" so I could watch and learn.'

Other early influences were Jackie Wilson, Sammy Davis Jr, the Motown artists and later, more surprisingly, the Bee Gees. Music was everywhere. Joe might not have been a professional musician himself, but he continued to play in private, something else that was to make an impression on his sons. One of the great tragedies of Michael's childhood was that his father wasn't as much of a beneficial influence as he should have been: after all, the two did have a lot in common. Joe, however, ruled not by encouraging love, but through fear.

In later life, Michael talked a great deal about the fear of his father, but he was capable of remembering happier times, too. 'This period for me which stands out is because I was so young around that time,' Michael told Jesse Jackson. 'I was like 8… 8 or 9. I just remember the environment, what it was like, all the music I was hearing. My father played guitar, my uncle played guitar. Every day they would come over, and you know they would play great music. And we would start to perform to the music.

'I remember seeing marching bands go down the street. I would remember the rhythm of the band and the beats of the drum. And every sound around me seems to record in my head and start making rhythms and dancing. I use to dance to the rhythm of the washing machine. My mother went to the corner store to wash the clothes. I would dance to the rhythm and people would crowd around; I remember those kind of stories. They would crowd around pretty much and watch me, those kind of little things.'

But while Michael's recollections in that interview were positive, life was far from idyllic back then. From the age of five, his life as a normal child was effectively over. Perhaps this was something that might have occurred anyway, given the massive weight of the stardom about to fall on his shoulders, but it was incalculably made worse by his father's behaviour.

Determined his sons would make it in a way that he himself never could, Joe instigated a regime that some would call barbaric. For a start, the boys were to call him Joe, never anything else. While not unkind in itself, this rather emphasised the professional aspect of his relationship to his sons was paramount. But that was nothing compared to what came next: Joe was harsh on all the children, but Michael, a particularly sensitive child, would take it especially to heart. Joe told him he was ugly, that he had a big nose – and it doesn't take Freud to see that this was sowing the seeds of a later obsession with plastic surgery. Worse still, he sometimes physically chastised his sons if ever they hit a duff note.

According to Michael's lifelong confidant J. Randy Taraborrelli, on one occasion Joe entered Michael's bedroom through an open window wearing a fright mask, screaming and shouting. He said this was to teach Michael not to leave his windows open; Michael later admitted it gave him nightmares for years to come.

Indeed, talking to Oprah Winfrey, he revealed that he was so frightened of his father that he would sometimes vomit when he saw him, something that continued into adulthood. In the other major interview he gave in his later years – the one that would ultimately lead to his destruction – he told TV journalist Martin Bashir in a documentary broadcast in February 2003, 'If you didn't do it the right way, he would tear you up, really get you.'

In later years, Joe Jackson attempted to dumb down some of the stories, although in truth, he probably succeeded only in making himself seem even harsher than his son had already described him. In 2003, he gave an interview with presenter Louis Theroux, in which he admitted some physical abuse, but denied it had gone as far as others suggested.

'I whipped him with a switch and a belt,' he admitted. 'I never beat him – you beat someone with a stick.' And as for claims that Michael would 'regurgitate' when he saw his father, Joe responded, 'He regurgitates all the way to the bank. That's right.' When asked about Michael's by-then extensive plastic surgery: 'He can do what he likes with his nose.' Of course, Michael could, and he did, but it was almost impossible not to conclude that Joe had no idea of the terrible damage he may have done to his son.

At that stage in his childhood, as he took over as lead singer of the Jackson 5 along with Jermaine, Michael was totally unaware of what a talent he had, being so young and knowing nothing else. As a child we naturally accept what is around us as the norm and at that point, not realising quite what a strange upbringing this was becoming, Michael thought his experience was the same as everyone else's.

'You know when you have a special ability,' he told Jesse Jackson. 'You don't realise it because you think everybody else has the same gift that you have, so you don't realise it. When I used to sing at such a young age, people were so inspired by my singing and they loved it. I didn't realise why they were clapping or crying, or starting to scream. I really, truly didn't, Jesse. And just later on in life, people would come up to me and say, "You know, do you realise you have a special gift?" or "you have a special talent."

'I just remember from my mother, who is very religious, always telling us to always thank God, to thank Jehovah God for your talent, your ability. You know, it's not from, it's not our doing, and it's from above, so we were always humbled by people who would come with accolades or you know, adulations or whatever it is. You know, it was a beautiful thing.'

It was not long before talk of the extraordinary new group, five brothers headed by an eight-year-old with an amazing voice, began to spread. Initially, the band played in local venues around Gary, Indiana, but soon achieved a reputation for excellence. From 1966 to 1968, they began touring extensively throughout the Midwest.

Often they would perform at nightspots known as the 'chitlin circuit', black clubs that were frequently striptease venues. No life for a child, it set down the marker for what was to be the norm for Michael, again reversing the natural order so that what might seem to most people to be extraordinary became the stuff of everyday, and vice versa.

'On stage for me was home,' Michael told Oprah Winfrey, and if truth be told, this set the pattern for the rest of his life. It was to be all he really knew: the acclaim and applause of the audience was something he both needed and feared as he made his way through life. Even then, it was beginning to take a terrible toll: 'I was most comfortable on stage, but once I got off, I was like, very sad... Lonely, sad, having to face popularity and all that... There were times when I had great times with my brothers, pillow-fights and things, but I used to always cry from loneliness.' That little bit older, his brothers were often far more interested in bedroom antics other than pillow fights.

In 1966, the Jackson 5 had the first of several breaks that would lead them to the very top of the show-business tree. With Michael on lead vocals – still just eight years old – the brothers won a major talent show, performing various Motown classics, and a James Brown song, 'I Got You (I Feel Good)'. This alerted various local record labels to the group and in 1967, they recorded several songs for Steeltown, including a number called 'Big Boy'. This was great for Michael's career, rather less so for his social development.

Much has been made of his lost childhood, not least by Michael himself, and already it was clear that his was to be a solitary life, dominated almost entirely by work. Michael had no friends of his own age: because he didn't go to school, opportunities were limited and the world in which he now lived was entirely an adult one. Sadly, he was to spend the rest of his life attempting to get his childhood back, something he would never succeed in doing.

'I would do my schooling – which was three hours with a tutor – and right after that, I would go to the recording studio and record, and I'd record for hours and hours until it was time to go to sleep,' Michael told Oprah. 'And I remember going to the record studio and there was a park across the street, and I'd see all the children playing and I would cry because it would make me sad that I would have to work instead.' But no one seemed to understand that the little boy was suffering so badly: as long as he was performing well and earning money – which he was – then as far as everyone else was concerned, all was well in his world.

Matters would soon intensify, because the group was about to make a massive breakthrough – and after that, there really was no turning back. In 1968, the Jackson 5 came to the attention of the Motown record label, probably still the most famous name for black artists worldwide. After some equivocation, they were snapped up. Jesse Jackson asked Michael who had initially discovered them for Motown – at the time it was put about that it had been Diana Ross. Although she and Michael would become close friends, this was not quite what happened back then.

'Well, in complete truth, it was Gladys Knight and a guy named Bobby Taylor,' Michael replied. 'And they were on the bill of some of the shows... you would do a show and there would be like, twenty or thirty acts. It was pretty much like Bonneville. You would do just a certain number of songs and you would go off. They were always on these shows. And they would watch us and they were so impressed with what we were doing. And Berry Gordy wasn't interested at first, but eventually he loved us and wanted to sign us.'

Bobby Taylor proved instrumental to the Jacksons' success. He was a performer and producer who had watched the act at The Regal nightclub in Chicago in 1968. Afterwards, he was insistent Berry Gordy should also see them perform. The first time Gordy saw the Jacksons, it was not actually live – rather, it was an audition tape – but this was enough to convince him that here was a group capable of stratospheric success.

It was then that the Diana Ross connection started: her enormous clout in the industry was put to use to launch the Jackson 5. 'After being signed, since Diana Ross was their biggest star at the time... he used her as the vehicle to introduce us to the public,' Michael continued. 'The first album was called *Diana Ross Presents the Jackson 5.*' The other, very important woman they met back then was Suzanne de Passe, creative assistant to Berry Gordy, who was responsible for nurturing the band, developing their act and even such necessities as helping to choose their outfits when they appeared on *The Ed Sullivan*

Show. She was one of the key figures to be responsible for their success.

In 1969, about a year after they'd signed with the label, the Jackson 5 was ready to go. That August a coming-out party was held in their honour at the Beverly Hills Club and a few days later, the band opened for the Supremes at the Los Angeles forum. Shortly afterwards their debut single, 'I Want You Back' was released and the world of show business was stunned. They caused a sensation. *Rolling Stone* magazine put Michael on the cover under the headline, 'Why does this 11-year-old stay up past his bedtime?' Inside, he was described as a 'prodigy' with 'overwhelming musical gifts'. The magazine noted that he, 'quickly emerged as the main draw and lead singer,' when performing with his brothers. *Rolling Stone* was right in every particular: from the very beginning, it was Michael who was clearly going to be the star.

All the seeds were being sown for what would make Michael Jackson great and yet destroy him in the end. Had anyone but known it, his story started as bubblegum pop and ended pretty much a Shakespearian tragedy. But the Jackson 5 was ready to go. Rarely has a group had such a spectacular debut: their first four singles all reached No. 1. They were: 'I Want You Back', 'ABC', 'The Love You Save' and 'I'll Be There'. Right from the word go, they were breaking records and

Michael was becoming, courtesy of that first single, the youngest-ever singer to get to No. 1.

'I Want You Back', released in 1969 from the album *Diana Ross Presents The Jackson 5*, summed up the strange life Michael now had. Originally intended for Gladys Knight and the Pips, and then for Diana Ross, under the title 'I Wanna Be Free', the song is about a lover who realises he shouldn't have ditched his partner – an adult theme, if ever there was one. When Michael sang it, he was just 11 years old – although the publicity people were allowing him to be thought even younger. It was to summarise a strange pattern in his life: as a child, he was plunged far too early into an adult world, while as an adult he spent the rest of his life trying to regain the status of a child.

All this was simply exacerbated by the success of the song. It reached No. 1 in the USA and No. 2 in the UK, sold 6 million copies, has been ranked 120 on *Rolling Stone*'s list of the 500 Greatest Songs Of All Time, number 9 on *Rolling Stone*'s 100 Greatest Pop Songs Since 1963 and cited by the *Daily Telegraph* as 'arguably the best pop music single of all time'.

But it also sealed Michael's fate. Now that both his father (by then very much the Jackson 5's manager) and Motown saw what a money-making machine the youngest Jackson had the potential to become, there was no way they would let their protégé do much else but work. And the public adored him from the word go. Fizzing with energy, bubbling with charm, Michael was a most engaging little boy, seemingly totally normal and happy in the world in which he now lived.

Meanwhile, massive changes and upheavals were afoot. For a start, Michael, his brothers and Joe began spending lengthy periods in LA, while Katherine and the other children remained behind in Gary. Michael was thus deprived not only of the company of other children but the home he had always known, as well as his mother, to whom he was exceptionally close. Enchanted as anyone to meet the new young sensation, Diana Ross took him under her wing, but this was no substitute for having his mother around. More isolated than ever, he was still so young and unable to comprehend what was going on. When he wasn't in the studio, he was spending all his time with big stars. For some time, his life hadn't had a great deal to do with the real world, but now he was increasingly cut off and alienated from the way the vast majority of people live.

Still, there was work to be done. The following year saw the release of the Jackson 5's next single, 'ABC', from the album of the same name. Like the earlier single, it was written and produced by The Corporation, which was made up of Motown royalty: Berry Gordy, Freddie Perren, Alphonzo Mizell and Deke Richards. 'ABC' was first heard on *American Bandstand* in 1970 and promptly knocked The Beatles' 'Let It Be' off the No. 1 slot. Michael would later become friends for a time with Paul McCartney – indeed, would record with him – but could not have imagined back in those days the relationship that was to ensue.

By now, the Jackson 5 was also heading 20,000-seater stadiums themselves. Their next single, 'The Love You Save' (also released in 1970), knocked another Beatles' number off the top slot, in this case, 'The Long And Winding Road'. Also written by The Corporation, it was another unusual song for a very young boy to sing, telling a 'fast' girl to slow down.

If anyone deemed this inappropriate for a small boy who hadn't yet reached puberty, then they were keeping quiet. By then, the cash tills were ringing loud and clear. Before they moved to LA, the entire Jackson clan squeezed into a small, two-bedroom house in Gary, Indiana. Now it seemed a real possibility that the family would become seriously rich on the back of its children's talent, especially Michael. In later years, Katherine was to reminisce that her happiest times had been while they were still together, all of them in that little house, before the Jackson 5 made it. Perhaps if they had stayed in that set-up, Michael might have thrived but, already, far too much was at stake for anyone to be overly concerned about that.

CHAPTER THREE

CHILD PRODIGY ON THE LOOSE

The final in that quartet of early singles, which established once and for all that the Jackson 5 were a serious force to be reckoned with, was 'I'll Be There'. Their most successful single ever, selling 4.2 million copies in the US and 6.1 million worldwide, for more than a decade it became the most successful Motown single ever, until it was dislodged by Diana Ross's 'Endless Love'. In fact, at the time, it knocked Marvin Gaye's 'I Heard It Through The Grapevine' off pole position.

This single was slightly different from the three that had gone before: for a start, it was a ballad, whereas the others were more bubblegum pop. Secondly, it was not the work of The Corporation but written and produced by Hal Davis, Willie Hutch and Bob West. It also marked a departure for Michael, in that he was now finding the confidence to ad lib. In the spoken line of the song, he implores his former lover to look over her shoulder to see that he will always be there for her. For some time, his showmanship had been apparent, but now so too was his confidence – professionally, at least – there was flair and joy in the performances that he was now turning in. He might not have had a clue about the real nature of the very adult emotions he was singing about, but he was certainly putting them across on stage.

Again, however, no one seemed to notice quite what an inappropriate song this was for someone of Michael's tender years. The singer asks his lover for a second chance, telling her that he'll be there to comfort her and he'll still be there for her, even if she eventually finds love with someone else. Allmusic.com states: 'Rarely, if ever, had one so young sung with so much authority and grace, investing this achingly tender ballad with wisdom and understanding far beyond his years.' Michael must have had no concept of what he was singing about, and in many ways, he never would, either. Cast adrift in an adult world, he would never go on to experience any proper emotional development, never undo the damage being done to him back then.

And it wasn't just that he was being asked to sing about subjects he didn't understand: he was witnessing them, too. In those days, the Jackson 5 pretty much divided their time between the recording studio and touring, and when they were out on the road, his brothers did what bands generally do: they brought groupies back to their room. The only problem was that Michael was present, witnessing these things.

His introduction to sex was seeing what his brothers got up to – and he was well aware of what his father was doing, too, come to that. Joe was as happy as the rest of them to chat up the groupies, which, to a gentle soul like Michael, who adored his mother, must have been hard to bear indeed. He was not torn between his parents, in that his mother was the one his loyalty lay towards, but to witness his father's behaviour and then have to return to Katherine, pretending nothing had happened, would not have been easy for anyone, let alone an 11-year-old. Not that the public got a whiff of this back then.

Michael Jackson was simply a massively talented and hugely charismatic youngster, talent fizzing out of his every pore. Lively and seemingly happy as Larry, he was merely another child star with a talent far beyond his years; at the time, no one realised what was going on behind the scenes, or that Michael was being treated much as a workhorse with the one hope of getting him to earn as much as he could. It was a tragedy waiting to happen – and it did.

Michael left school very young, at which stage he was then tutored privately. From that moment on, he was completely cut off from the world, with no idea what normal standards of behaviour were or how people acted towards one another. He was, after all, immersed in Planet Showbiz, a place markedly different from any kind of normal behaviour, let alone a suitable environment in which to bring up a child. The reason why Michael Jackson, the adult, seemed so cut off from reality is because that is precisely what happened to Michael Jackson, the child.

And now, spending his time almost entirely with other performers, and with no other child with whom to compare notes, Michael had no conception that he stood out from the crowd. He had no idea his talent was unusual, nor indeed that he was so markedly different.

As Michael's popularity continued to soar, at Motown the powers that be started to realise that he had the potential not only to front the Jackson 5, but also to hold down a solo career. Ultimately, his solo work would far outshine anything he did with the Jackson 5, but even back then, just into his teens, he branched out alone. Between 1972 and 1975, he released four albums with the label, on top of which, of course, there was work to be done with the rest of his family, along with the incessant touring. It was a workload that would have shattered an adult performer, let alone one who would more conventionally at this age have been attending school.

The two albums that stand out from this period, both

of which also produced singles with the same title, are: *Got To Be There* and *Ben*. *Got To Be There* featured the young Michael on its cover, grinning broadly, a cap pressing down on his Afro. Seeing that carefree photo, no one would ever have dreamed of the life he was leading behind the scenes. The album contained a number of cover versions, including 'Ain't No Sunshine', 'Rockin' Robin' and 'You've Got A Friend'; the title track, meanwhile, was written by Elliot Willensky. Michael's first solo single came out in 1971, reaching No. 4 on the Billboard Charts. Though not quite the chart success of the songs recorded with his brothers, it was enough to let the record label know that, clearly, he had a future as a singer in his own right.

By now, the family had relocated to a large compound in Encino, California, where Michael would remain until his mid-twenties. The Jacksons still spent a huge amount of time out on the road, but at least their home base was in the heart of the industry, and although Michael was away a lot, when he was in LA, he could still be with his mother. In an increasingly strange world, Katherine remained one of the few points of stability: Michael and his brothers had now started to achieve that level of fame where life can become very difficult. There was the constant attention, the autograph hunters, the feeling that everyone wanted a piece of him, the knowledge that everything he did was watched.

Opinion varies as to which is Michael Jackson's best single, but there is a camp who opt for 'Billie Jean', with its overtones of paranoia and mistrust, and many of those emotions started to appear way back then. Michael was now becoming public property on a massive scale, and there was nothing that anyone could do to stop this; nor, indeed, did anyone want to. His sufferings as a child were real enough, but they were hidden from almost everyone. To the outside world, and to everyone at his record label, he was the child prodigy, the little boy with the cherubic grin, the great voice and an almost ludicrously strong aptitude for dance.

Behind the scenes, however, the constant work and touring was as much of a burden as it ever had been. The group was now internationally famous, which meant not only were they touring the US, but the rest of the world, as well. Many adult artists have a hard time coping with fame, but Michael was still only a child and the pressures being brought to bear on him seemed intolerable at the time.

'Well, I loved show business and I still love show business, but then there are times you just want to play and have some fun, and that part did make me sad,' he admitted to Oprah Winfrey in the 1993 interview with her. 'I remember one time we were getting ready to go to South America and everything was packed up and in the car ready to go, and I hid and I was crying because I really did not want to go; I wanted to play, I did not want to go.'

Around this time Michael faced competition for the first time, when it came to teen singing sensation, and for a short while, his rival actually won. Donny Osmond was also part of a large family, five brothers who made up a band, The Osmonds. Like Michael, Donny had begun to stand out from the rest, although he was not the group's lead singer (that was Merrill) and he, too, was being groomed for a solo career. The two, who were also about the same age, pretty much went head to head in the early seventies, and their labels followed similar tactics, too: both were releasing old fifties' numbers, in Donny's case, 'Puppy Love' (MGM Records), while Michael had a huge hit with 'Rockin' Robin' in 1971.

Both boys were subjected to strict regimes by severely controlling fathers, although there the resemblance ended. When the journalist Virginia Blackburn interviewed Donny Osmond in 2001, she asked how he managed to emerge from child stardom in much better shape than Michael. 'My father wasn't Joe Jackson,' he simply replied.

'Rockin' Robin', originally a Bobby Day number from 1958, got to No. 2 in the charts and was the perfect vehicle for Michael's talents: a rollicking number designed to get everyone up on the dance floor, as his truly great singles would do just under a decade hence. The comparison to a mini-James Brown was never more apt, as Michael spun round, microphone in hand, belting it out with a maturity that far belied his tender years. Marlon provided background vocals, but now Michael was increasingly separated from his brothers – it was clear that some day soon there would be a split.

But not back then, and meanwhile, the rivalry with the new kids on the block intensified. At the time, there was sneering in some quarters to the effect that The Osmonds were a white version of the Jackson 5, only launching themselves on the back of their rivals' ongoing success. This was not entirely fair, given that they had, if anything, been around even longer than the Jacksons, with all four starting out as a barbershop quartet in 1958, but there was certainly some crossover in their music. Indeed, The Osmonds' hit 'One Bad Apple' might have been written for the Jackson 5, with Joe reportedly furious that the other camp got to it first and his boys had missed out. Both groups certainly benefited from their youngest members, who would outshine their brothers and embark on a solo career. Donny's career might have been as successful as Michael's, but in most other ways, he enjoyed a far happier life.

Again, there were more similarities, and differences, between the two. Like Michael, Donny had been performing since he was little more than a toddler, but the real difference was that at that time, Donny was a heartthrob, something Michael definitely could not be described as being. Massively popular, certainly, and an accredited talent, really far more than Donny, Michael was not a singer that young girls swooned over; he was someone they thought cute, fun and a great singer, but that was that. And to a certain extent, that was always the way it was going to be.

Of course, Michael had millions of fans who found him deeply attractive, especially around the period of his physical heyday, in his late teens and early twenties, but his fame stemmed not from the fact that fans were eager to sleep with him, rather they wanted to dance to his music and see him perform. In many ways, for all the groundbreaking work he did, Michael made it simply because he was an old fashioned all-round entertainer, a song-and-dance man, just, in his case, to the power of 10.

Back then, neither boy was ever the subject of sex scandal, although sadly this wasn't to prove so in Michael's later years. In Donny's case his family were strict Mormons and he has publicly disclosed his only partner in his life has been his wife; for Michael, opportunity was everywhere, but he just wasn't interested.

He was still forced to witness his brothers with groupies while out on tour, which would almost certainly have filled a boy as young as himself with distaste. It is hardly surprising that Michael was never able to form a proper long-term relationship with a woman, given how he was introduced to love and sex in his early life. He even warned some girls to stay away from his brothers, warnings that all too often went unheeded.

Indeed, most of the women he would become close to were much older, mother figures: Diana Ross, Elizabeth Taylor and, to a lesser extent, Jane Fonda. Even Grace Rwaramba, nanny to his own children for 17 years until Michael and she parted company in December 2008, had a slightly maternal relationship with him; she was actually eight years his junior, but looked after him in much the same way as she did the youngsters. Michael didn't want a girlfriend, and he certainly didn't want a groupie: he wanted his mother, but she was thousands of miles away.

Somewhat appropriately, Michael's next single was a love song – to a rat. Originally written for Donny Osmond by Don Black and Walter Sharf, Donny was on tour at the time and therefore unable to record, so that honour duly went to Michael. There is some irony in all this: despite the fact that Donny had the edge over Michael back then he would soon lose it permanently. When twenty-something Donny asked twenty-something Michael what he might do to revive his flagging career, the latter's answer was, 'Change your name.' While the two were always on amicable terms, it's hard not to conclude that someone as competitive as Michael would become couldn't help but be secretly pleased about the turn of events.

'Ben' was the theme song of a movie of the same name released in 1972, the sequel to *Willard* (1971), about a killer rat. It did extremely well, becoming Michael's first solo No. 1 in the States and making it to No. 7 in the UK. Records began being broken again: Michael became the third youngest solo artist to have a No. 1 – Stevie Wonder had pole position, getting there with 'Fingertips, Pt. 2' when he was just 13, while Donny Osmond was not quite 14 when he achieved the No. 2 slot with 'Go Away Little Girl'. 'Ben' eventually won a Golden Globe for Best Song and was nominated for an Academy Award for Best Original Song in 1973. Michael performed it at the Academy Awards ceremony that year: he was, by now, 14.

Because he was around adults all the time, in many ways Michael was now treated as an adult himself. He was beginning to understand the music business as well as any forty-something, developing a shrewdness that would stand him in very good stead a decade hence. It was in part because he appeared, outwardly, to be developing into not just a superb performer, but a canny businessman too that, again, no one realised what was really happening to the now adolescent boy. During the 1993 interview with Oprah, she reminded him that Smokey Robinson, among numerous others, commented that Michael was an old soul in a young body, to which he concurred.

'I remember hearing that all the time when I was little,' he admitted. 'They used to call me a 45-year-old midget wherever I went. I just used to hear that and wherever I went... Just like when some people said when you were little and you started to sing, did you know you were that good? And I say I never thought about it, I just did it and it came out. I never thought about it.' Indeed not. Back then Michael was doing pretty much exactly as he was told.

However, he was developing a pretty sharp nose for what did (and didn't) work in the music industry, as indeed were his brothers, and by the mid-1970s, the relationship with Motown started to sour. From about 1973 onwards, sales of their records began to falter and although they still produced hits such as 'Dancing Machine' and 'I Am Love', seemingly they were no longer guaranteed success with every move they made. But when the Jacksons themselves, along with Joe, approached Motown with a view to having a greater say over their output, they were turned down flat. Motown was Motown, after all.

Except by this time, the Jacksons had established a fair bit of clout in the industry: money talks, and they were making a lot of it. There was no shortage of other record labels interested in taking them on, and so in 1975, the group left Motown and signed to CBS Records, in the Philadelphia International Records division, later renamed Epic Records.

The move heralded some other changes, too. For a start, they were no longer legally permitted to use the name 'Jackson 5' any more, and so they renamed themselves, The Jacksons. It was a move created out of necessity, but it seemed symbolic, too: a new name for a new era. The Jacksons had a more mature ring than that teenbop outfit, the Jackson 5. At the time, the line-up also changed: Jermaine left to forge a solo career with Motown, while Randy stepped into his place. Various hits followed, most notably 'Blame It On The Boogie'.

Jermaine's departure was the start of one of numerous family rifts the Jacksons have endured over the years. Like Michael, he had been forging ahead with a successful solo career while still singing within the family, starting with the 1972 Shep & The Limelite's cover, 'Daddy's Home'. But when Michael started singing with the group, Jermaine was left slightly marginalised; previously he had been lead vocalist, a role he now had to share, when he was able to take the lead at all. By the time the Jacksons left Motown, his role had diminished to the extent that he was barely singing lead at all, factors that would have been instrumental in him deciding on a solo career.

There was another factor at play too: Jermaine was

married to Berry Gordy's daughter. He and Hazel Gordy tied the knot in 1973, and they went on to have three children: Jermaine Jr (usually called Jay), a daughter (Autumn) and another son, Jaimy. Ultimately, the marriage would not stand the test of time – they divorced in 1987 – but Jermaine was faced with a stark choice when his brothers walked: did he go with them and upset his father-in-law, or stay and upset his brothers? In the end, he chose the latter option and had a relatively successful career for some years ahead.

In so doing, his actions created a family rift and the tensions between Michael and Jermaine would last for years. Much later, towards the end of Michael's life, when he was going through all his troubles with the court case, Jermaine would prove one of his staunchest supporters, turning up at the courtroom every day. But back then, when they all had the world at their feet and no inkling of the troubles awaiting them in the years ahead, Michael and Jermaine were rivals, both in the group and later, in their solo careers.

Michael told Oprah Winfrey that he didn't believe his brothers were envious of him, but they wouldn't have been human had they not noticed quite how exceptionally well their younger brother seemed to be doing compared to the rest of them, not to mention his massive appropriation of the limelight. Ultimately, tragedy and drama would reunite them all.

Another enormous change that took place around then was that Michael started to write the songs that the group performed. Tastes were changing: disco was becoming increasingly popular and this began to be reflected in the music put out by the band. These are classic tracks that remain hugely popular: 'Shake Your Body (Down To The Ground)', 'This Place Hotel' and 'Can You Feel It' were all huge hits, and a whole new sound for the group. Meanwhile, Michael was now verging on adulthood: his voice had broken, although he retained the soft falsetto that was to be his trademark throughout his career. He had grown into a handsome young man, albeit one who had still never been linked to any woman in the public eye, and on the cover of 'Shake Your Body (Down to The Ground)', all five sported massive Afros, very much the fashion of the day.

But that dangerous obsession with his appearance was taking hold. In his late teens, Michael suffered from acne, which made him hugely self-conscious, so much so that he went through periods when he didn't want anyone to see him. Joe did not help: he teased his son about his appearance. 'I had pimples so badly it used to make me so shy,' Michael confided in Oprah. 'I used not to look at myself. I'd hide my face in the dark, I wouldn't want to look in the mirror and my father teased me, and I just hated it and I cried every day.'

There was also the problem of growing up. Ultimately,

of course, Michael's past as a child star would catch up with him to tragic effect. But at the time, unlike his near rival Donny Osmond, he was to make a highly successful transition from teen sensation to adult superstar. However, during those crucial teenage years, frequently miserable for anyone, and exacerbated for Michael by isolation and fear of his father, to say nothing of a growing self-loathing when it came to his own appearance, there was yet something else to contend with: the knowledge that some parts of his fan base didn't want him to change. In fact, they didn't want him to grow up at all. But how could anyone stop that? Michael later went on to become preoccupied with a fear of ageing. Little wonder: it was already an issue when he wasn't even out of his teens.

'I think every child star suffers through this period because you're not the cute and charming child that you were,' Michael revealed to Oprah. 'You start to grow, and they want to keep you little forever. And, um, nature takes its course.'

But unlike Donny, whose fans just could not bear to see him turn into a grown man, Michael's would ultimately be able to accept it. His music helped, too. The first single that he wrote for The Jacksons, 'Shake Your Body (Down To The Ground)', from the album *Destiny*, was a massive hit. He actually co-wrote the song with Randy. It got to No. 7 on the Billboard Hot

100 main chart and reached No. 3 on the Billboard R&B Singles chart. Eventually, the record would sell over 2 million copies, attaining double platinum status from the Recording Industry Association of America (RIAA). Sadly, this was to be the very last song performed live by The Jacksons as a group, at the Michael Jackson 30th Anniversary concert held in New York's Madison Square Garden in September 2001.

The next single, 'This Place Hotel' (originally intended as 'Heartbreak Hotel'), was released in 1980 from the *Triumph* album. Michael was the only Jackson singing, but the others played percussion (in Tito's case, guitar). The song reached 22 on the Billboard pop singles chart and No. 2 on the R&B singles chart. It would become a very popular number during live performances and Michael continued to sing it well into his solo career.

And then came 'Can You Feel It', the following year: 1981. Although in some ways not so successful as the songs that preceded it, getting to 77 on the pop charts and 30 on the R&B charts, it did better in the UK, where it reached No. 6. In many ways, this was the most memorable of the trio. Co-written by Michael and Jackie, it opens with that very distinctive riff that would usher an entire generation onto the dance floor, simultaneously spreading the message that world peace is a great thing to aim for, that it was a good time to dance.

But what really made it stand out was the

extraordinary accompanying video, directed by Bruce Gowers and Robert Abel. Back then, the music video was still in its infancy, this being the year that MTV started, but the work was massively ahead of its time. Opening with a speech about renewing the earth, the brothers seem almost god-like figures, translucent and towering above. Against images of rebirth and regeneration, Michael variously appears to be the font of a river of fire, before pushing a rainbow above his head. Meanwhile, crowds (many of them children, all bathed in the golden light of fire), look on in wonderment. It was like nothing anyone had ever seen before, and in 2001 was voted one of the top 100 music videos of all time in a poll to mark MTV's twentieth anniversary. ('Thriller' came second, narrowly trounced by Fatboy Slim's 'Praise You'.)

Meanwhile, Michael had been involved in other projects. Like Donny and Marie Osmond, The Jacksons got their own TV show, a variety programme showcasing not only their own talents, but those of their guests too. Starting off as a one-off special in 1976, the producers were so pleased they commissioned more programmes. Now the entire Jackson family (with the exception of Jermaine, who was off at Motown) was introduced to the world. Janet Jackson, who would go on to cultivate massive fame in her own right, had already appeared in public as a child actress, but now she and the slightly older La Toya performed with their brothers for the very first time.

Between the song and dance routines, there were comedy sketches with the guests, who included a very young David Letterman, as well as the likes of Dom DeLuise, Muhammad Ali, Sonny Bono and Tina Turner. Good showcase as it was for their talents, though, the series only lasted one season before it was taken off-air. At that point, the band's reputation was slightly in decline, one of the reasons why it didn't really take off.

At the tail end of the seventies, the other major project that Michael became involved with was his first movie, *The Wiz*, for which he decamped to New York with La Toya in October 1977. Released in 1978, the film was a reworking of *The Wizard Of Oz* with an all-black cast: the role of Dorothy went to his friend and mentor Diana Ross, while he himself played the Scarecrow. Nipsey Russell was the Tin Man and the Cowardly Lion played by Ted Ross.

The action moves from Kansas to New York, and the story follows the original fairly closely: Dorothy enlists her friends to take her to the Emerald City (an analogue of the real-life World Trade Center plaza), encountering all sorts of obstacles along the way, such as the Subway Peddlar and his evil puppets as well as the Poppy Girls, prostitutes who attempt to put our heroes to sleep. A veritable Who's Who of African American actors appeared in the film: Mabel King, Theresa Merritt, Thelma Carpenter, Lena Horne and Richard Pryor made up just some of the cast.

Produced by Motown Productions and Universal Pictures, the film cost what was at the time a stratospheric $24 million to make. Critically and commercially, it was also a resounding flop, although attitudes towards it have softened over the years. Diana Ross lobbied intensively for the role, but at 33, many felt that she was perhaps a bit too old to play a 16-year-old. In fact, some critics considered it effectively ended her movie career. The script, according to the book *Mr. and Mrs. Hollywood*, was 'too scary for children and too silly for adults.' All in all, it was a mess.

One person stood out from all the drubbing: Michael. He had taken his role extremely seriously, spending hours watching videos of gazelles, cheetahs and panthers, so that he might emulate their graceful movements. His make-up alone took five hours to apply each day. The critics were much kinder to him, remarking that he possessed, 'genuine acting talent' and 'provided the only memorable moments.' As so often in his life, the meticulous preparation he put in paid off. Michael himself was resolutely upbeat, insisting, 'I don't think it could have been any better, I really don't,' adding that the film was, 'my greatest experience so far – I'll never forget that.' The set design came in for some praise too, and *The Wiz* was nominated for four Oscars, although it didn't receive any of them: Best Art Direction, Best Costume Design, Best Original Music Score and Best Cinematography.

Sadly, Michael would never develop much more of an acting career, limiting himself to the likes of *Moonwalker*, a collection of short films and extended music videos. But it had been an interesting experience and also his first opportunity to work with a man who was to change his life.

Quincy Jones was the musical supervisor and music producer on the movie, an experience he did not particularly enjoy, saying later that he only did it for director Sidney Lumet. But he was very impressed with Michael, later comparing his work and dedication to Sammy Davis Jnr. Indeed, so enamoured was he that he decided the two of them should do some work together, work that would change the face of popular entertainment. To this day, it remains Michael's greatest achievement.

Around the time that Quincy Jones and Michael started work on what would become some of the most definitive albums of the eighties, another life-changing event occurred. Michael had an accident that required an operation on his nose, leading him to a discovery that would have devastating consequences. Now he could change the shape of his face.

CHAPTER FOUR

MICHAEL JACKSON – SUPERSTAR

Quincy Delight Jones Jr is an institution. These days, he's the granddaddy of American rock and pop. A music conductor, record producer, musical arranger, film composer and trumpeter, the American impresario has had 79 Grammy Award recommendations, a record 27 Grammy Awards, including the Grammy Legend Award in 1991, and in 1968 he became the first African American, along with his song-writing partner Bob Russell, to be nominated for an Oscar for Best Original Song. That year, he also became the first African American to be nominated twice within the same year when he received a nomination for his work on the 1967 movie, *In Cold Blood*.

Numerous other awards and records are attached to his name. He originated a brand new sound with the instrumental 'Soul Bossa Nova' in 1962 and has been involved with numerous films from an early Woody Allen, *Take The Money and Run* to *Austin Powers: International Man of Mystery*. In 1971 he became the first African American to be named musical director/conductor at the Oscars. He was the first, and to this date, only, African American to be nominated as a producer for Best Picture for *The Color Purple* (1986); also, the first African American to win the Jean Hersholt Humanitarian Award in 1995. Along with Willie D. Burton, the two hold the record for being the most Oscar-nominated African American, with a tally of seven nominations each.

Quincy has also worked extensively with Frank Sinatra, been married three times and had a lengthy relationship with the German actress Nastassja Kinski, while fathering seven children along the way. Born in Chicago in 1933, he is a social activist and does a huge amount of charity work for South Africa and Brazil. In Jewish circles, he would be described as a 'mensch', a person of integrity and honour.

In short, both personally and professionally, Quincy Jones was the ideal person for Michael to work with, for while the singer tended to form friendships with much older women in the search for a mother figure, in many ways, he needed a father figure, too. Michael has publicly forgiven Joe and declared his love for him; the two were never extensively formally estranged despite the problems between them, although there were certainly long periods of non-communication. Joe remained Michael's manager at that time, but in Quincy Jones he found an older man who could help and guide him, with encouragement this time, rather than threats. Quite possibly, this would be the most successful partnership ever to have existed in the world of pop.

Michael and Quincy met on the set of *The Wiz* at a time when Michael was beginning to realise that he needed change in his career. The group's star was fading, although in truth they would manage to stay together for a few more years, and although the great disco sounds they were putting together back then have come to be regarded as classics, at the time they weren't actually doing very well. When he and his brothers first signed up to Motown, they churned out one No. 1 hit after another. But now a slot in the Top 20 wasn't guaranteed: clearly, something had to be done.

Quincy's reputation went before him and when he and Michael first met, they immediately hit it off. Consummate professionals, they recognised in each other kindred spirits, a desire to break boundaries and do what no other professional artists had managed to do before. The result of their collaboration was to be success on a scale never previously experienced, and still unmatched to this day.

Michael had, by now, been a solo artist as well as lead singer with The Jacksons for the best part of a decade, but he knew he must develop if his career was to have longevity. He asked Quincy for a recommendation as producer, Quincy recommended himself, and so musical history was made. So began the *Off The Wall* era, from 1978 to 1981. The first decisions to be made were the songs themselves. There were, quite literally, hundreds to choose from, but given both knew this was to be an absolutely crucial and defining moment in Michael's career, the selection process was strict. Only the very best material would get a look-in, with the result that four singles were released off the album (five, counting one in the UK), another record in itself.

Gradually, Michael had been coming into his own as a songwriter and he was really reaching a level of maturity now. Some of the material on the album was written by him including, 'Don't Stop Till You Get Enough' and 'Workin' Day and Night'. He also co-wrote 'Get On The Floor' with Louis Johnson. As for the rest of the tracks, some of the biggest names in showbiz contributed to *Off The Wall*. They included Paul McCartney, who wrote 'Girlfriend', Carole Bayer Sager's 'It's The Falling In Love', a duet Michael performed with Patti Austen, and Stevie Wonder co-wrote 'I Can't Help It'.

Rod Temperton was a very important presence on the album. He wrote 'Rock With You', 'Off The Wall' and

'Burn This Disco Out'. Originally, Michael and Quincy had intended to use just one of the songs, but in the event, they liked them so much that they included all three. Meanwhile, some years earlier Tom Bahler had written a number called 'She's Out Of My Life' for Quincy Jones. Michael heard it, loved it and was granted permission to use it on the album. It was very different from most of the songs he had been accustomed to performing, and his rendition proved just how far he had progressed as an artist. It revealed a whole new face of Michael Jackson to the world.

Between December 1978 and June 1979, the album was recorded at Allen Zentz Recording, Westlake Recording Studios and Cherokee Studios in LA. Mixing was done by Bruce Swedien, an engineer who was previously a Grammy Award winner himself. Following this, the tapes were sent to A&M Recording Studio for mastering. Meanwhile, given this was a new departure for Michael, careful thought was paid to the cover. In the event, Michael was pictured, still with an Afro (albeit rather more modest than the ones previously sported), wearing a tuxedo, thumbs in trouser pockets, but still ready to take to the dance floor.

In the event, this was to be one of the last major images of Michael while he still looked as nature decreed. An accident in 1979, while performing a dance routine to promote the album, introduced him to the concept of plastic surgery. It was to develop into an obsession, although at that stage no one dreamed that this good-looking black boy could possibly have had any issues with the way he looked.

And so to *Off The Wall* itself: while *Thriller* is often seen as the album that took Michael Jackson into a whole new league, in reality it was *Off The Wall* that totally changed his image and the way he was perceived. Disco was sexy and so, despite the childlike qualities still hanging over him, he was its new practitioner. Michael had not yet reached the crotch-grabbing stage of his dancing career, but his moves on stage were increasingly suggestive, calculated to whip an audience of young women into a frenzy – and so it did.

When the album was released, the reception was sensational. Michael had come of age. Any doubts that here was a child star, trying in vain to be taken seriously as an adult, were totally dispelled: both public and critics loved it. *Rolling Stone* magazine talked about Michael's 'breathless dreamy stutter' as being akin to that of Stevie Wonder. 'Jackson's feathery-timbered tenor is extraordinarily beautiful,' it went on. 'It slides smoothly into a startling falsetto that's used very daringly.' Indeed, those trademark gasps and shrieks, while in the pipeline for some time now, really came into their own in *Off The Wall*.

Stephen Holden of *Rolling Stone* certainly thought so.

'Like many an aging child star, Michael Jackson has had to grow up gracefully in public in order to survive,' he wrote in a review dated 1 November 1979. 'Until now, he's understandably clung to the remnants of his original Peter Pan of Motown image while cautiously considering the role of the young prince. *Off The Wall* marks Jackson's first decisive step toward a mature show-business personality, and except for some so-so material, it's a complete success.'

The work stood the test of time, too. In 2001, David O'Donnell wrote for the BBC, '1979's *Off The Wall* is one of the finest pop albums ever made and showcases Michael Jackson as a gifted and versatile vocalist, comfortable performing on ballads as well as upbeat disco tracks.' It certainly did. There was a depth and knowingness to Michael's performance that had not been there before, one that spoke of great things ahead.

When *Off The Wall* was released, the public loved it. Little Michael Jackson, that five-year-old prodigy, had turned into a mature, adult entertainer capable of entertaining the masses in a way rarely seen before. The album shot to No. 3 in the US charts and No. 1 on the US Soul Disco Chart, staying in the Top 20 for a phenomenal 48 weeks. The first single from the album was Michael's own number, 'Don't Stop Till You Get Enough', featuring a spoken intro, percussion from Randy and a snappy accompanying video. It flew to No.

1 in the States and Australia, hitting the Top 10 in six more countries.

'Don't Stop Till You Get Enough' is a remarkably exuberant work with a polished accompanying video directed by Nick Saxon, again hinting at what was to come. Michael hadn't quite got to the uniform as costume stage of his career and so he appeared in a tuxedo, with that soft breathy intro, talking about how he was about to dance, until bursting into his routine with aplomb, a cry of joy and striking a pose, a technique he would so often use in the future. He dances by himself and then with himself, literally, as two more Michael Jacksons join him halfway through, while the sheer charm and pizzazz of the piece are totally engaging.

The dancing is remarkable. Michael appears to be not so much at one with the music as to be the music itself: his body becomes fluid, producing the sound as much as responding to it. This has been described as his first 'story' video: in truth, it's not and that honour most probably goes to 'Can You Feel It'. But it is entirely polished, utterly Michael. And the spoken intro mirrors both 'Can You Feel It' in the past and 'Thriller' in the future – although in both these other cases, someone else was doing the talking. Meanwhile, Michael continued to develop the basics of so much that would shortly come along.

The single 'Don't Stop Till You Get Enough' was out in July 1979, followed by the album a month later, but something else momentous happened that month, too. Michael's 21st birthday was on 29 August 1979, which meant that, at long last, he was free from his father. His contract with Joe's management company, Joseph Jackson Productions, lapsed and was not renewed. There could be few who had witnessed the early years who would blame him and now he was free to take on someone else to handle his affairs. That person was John Branca, one of the foremost entertainment lawyers in the USA. 'I want to be the biggest star in show business – and the wealthiest,' Michael told him. As the old adage goes, be careful what you wish for. Most certainly, Michael would get his wish.

To a world unaware of quite what a hard childhood he had endured, the full implications of the move were not entirely apparent. It made the news, all right, Michael Jackson firing his father, but given the sheer joy he somehow managed to radiate whenever he was in public, no one knew of the misery going on behind the scenes. For Michael, this was a massive turning point. Not only had he transformed himself into a successful adult performer, he had also broken away from someone who had dominated his life in a dreadful way. Every young man must finally make the break with their male parent, but in some cases, it's more imperative than others. In many ways, Michael paid tribute to his father, admitting the discipline imposed by him meant that he learned to be as professional as possible. The downside of the relationship, however, was so great that only a break could start to give him the distance he needed. Alas, ultimately, this would not prove to be enough.

But certainly, all that wasn't obvious back then. *Off The Wall* was now turning into one of the year's major success stories, with one single after another rolling off the production line. 'Rock With You', followed in November, with another snappy video, this time directed by Bruce Gowers, with Michael prancing about in a sequined outfit, complete with matching boots. It, too, got to No. 1. The next single, released in the spring of 1980, was 'Off The Wall' itself. It made the Top Five in the US and the Top Ten in another four countries, followed by the haunting ballad 'She's Out Of My Life', with a video also directed by Bruce Gowers.

It is a very unusual video for Michael, in that there is no dancing at all: he merely sits on a stool, in the grand old tradition of torch singers, including Frank Sinatra, Sammy Davis Jr and just about every other twentieth-century American great, bewailing the lost love that would never be returned. Michael's performance was a very emotional one: there was real pain in his eyes, and Gowers kept reshooting as the singer continued to break down. Eventually, the emotion was left in.

So, why was this? Why was Michael clearly so genuinely moved by the tale of a man who had found love, only to lose it again? The publicity machine spun into action: it was claimed Michael had been dating Tatum O'Neal, herself a former child star and the daughter of actor Ryan O'Neal, and was distressed by the end of the relationship. In the infamous 2003 interview with TV journalist Martin Bashir. The star related that Tatum had once tried to seduce him, a claim she later denied. Whatever the truth, it is safe to say Michael had not been in love.

At that stage, he had never had a girlfriend and if there ever was a lost love of his own from that point in his life, they have never been discovered to this day. Far more likely was that Michael was beginning to have a sense of what he himself had lost: not love, but true peace of mind. He might have managed to rid himself of his father on one level, but the taunts he was forced to endure would stay with him until the end of his days. Just as his career was about to take off into the stratosphere, somehow Michael seemed to know that he would never be like everyone else.

It is interesting to note that the clothes he wears in some of the videos from that time, especially 'She's Out Of My Life', in which he is clad in a super-normal shirt and sweater, would be some of the last times he appeared in what looked like ordinary outfits. Soon, the military costumes would appear: the leathers of 'Thriller', the white suits of 'Billie Jean'. Here, his trousers are still a normal length, but they would shortly be hoisted up to reveal his ankles. Never again would Michael attempt to look just like everyone else. In fact, since his death, endless features have appeared in fashion magazines analysing the effect that his changing images had on style.

Off The Wall became the third-best-selling album of 1980. Michael won his first Grammy as a solo performer for Best R&B Performance for 'Don't Stop Till You Get Enough', while at the American Music Awards he won Favourite Soul Album, Favourite Male Artist and Favourite Soul Single for 'Don't Stop Till You Get Enough'. On top of this, he collected four Billboard Awards. By the following year, 1981, he had broken more records still: by then *Off The Wall* had sold 5 million copies and would ultimately notch up sales of 20 million. In addition, this was the first time that any artist managed to release four top-selling singles from just one album.

Everyone was thrilled, with one exception – Michael. He felt he hadn't done anything like as well as he'd hoped, telling John Branca, 'It was totally unfair that it didn't get and it can never happen again.[sic]' Matters were made worse by what he saw as a perceived snub by *Rolling Stone*. When he asked if the magazine would be

Above: Diana Ross took Michael under her wing when he was a young boy away from home with the band. They remained great friends.

Below: With Paul and Linda McCartney. Michael and Paul collaborated on songs such as 'Say Say Say' and 'The Girl Is Mine'.

Michael was a great animal lover. He is pictured, *above*, with his pet llama and Bubbles the chimp.

Below: Michael was at the top of his game with the release of *Thriller*, the biggest-selling album of all time.

Above: The debut of the Moonwalk. Michael unveiled what would become his signature move in March 1983 at the 'Motown 25' television special.

Below left: The famous red leather 'Thriller' outfit.

Below right: Michael with his friend and fellow former child star, Elizabeth Taylor.

In 1984, Michael was honoured with a Walk of Fame star on Hollywood Boulevard. His outfit for the day included his trademark sequinned white glove.

Jackomania! Mobbed by fans and photographers on a visit to London in 1985.

Setting the stage on fire during his *Bad* World Tour from 1987–1989, one of the most successful live tours of all time.

Above: Michael co-wrote the charity single 'We are the World' with Lionel Richie.

Below: Sophia Loren was one of the stars who paid tribute to her friend Michael after his death.

Above: In 1986, Michael starred in *Captain Eo*, a futuristic 3D film directed by Francis Ford Coppola (pictured *right*).

Below: Meeting Princess Diana after breaking a Guinness World Record for tour attendance at Wembley Stadium.

interested in doing a cover story on him, they turned him down. 'I've been told over and over that black people on the cover of magazines doesn't sell copies... Just wait,' he said. 'Someday those magazines are going to be begging me for an interview. Maybe I'll give them one, and maybe I won't.'

Of course, 10 years previously Michael had appeared on the cover of *Rolling Stone*, so it was clearly an unfair remark to make about the magazine, but this only added to a grievance that black artists were treated differently from white ones in the business he wanted to dominate.

He talked to Jesse Jackson about that time. 'Well, one of the great high points, I would have to say... I had done an album called *Off The Wall*. It was an important point for me because I had just [done] the movie *The Wiz* and I wanted to express myself as a writer, as an artist. You know, to write my own music, do the music, pretty much put it together. And Quincy Jones, who I've loved – I was fortunate to work with him and I love this man, he is very gifted. But I was writing these songs at the time, "Don't Stop Till You Get Enough", you know, "Shake Your Body to The Ground", you know "Billie Jean", and "Beat It" – you know, all those songs were written at this time.

'So, I pretty much was setting mental goals of what I want to do as an artist and it was a high point for me, during the winning of the Grammys for the *Off The*

Wall album, but I wasn't happy. Because I wanted to do much more than that... I wasn't happy with the way it was accepted. Even though it was a huge success, it was the biggest-selling album for a solo artist at that time – it was over 10 million, for a black solo artist! And I said for the next album, I refuse for them to ignore, and that's when I set my heart on writing the *Thriller* album.'

There it was again: Michael felt that being black was holding his career back. Nor was he being paranoid: at the time, MTV showed very few videos of black artists, something that would change when *Thriller* came along. That conviction that being black was holding him back only added to the self-loathing he already felt, especially towards his own appearance. It was a dangerous combination. And finally, in 1979, an event occurred that would trigger a dangerous obsession to remain with him until the end of his life: Michael accidentally broke his nose.

It happened when he was rehearsing a dance routine. Michael was rushed to hospital and had his first-ever plastic surgery, albeit out of necessity. The operation, however, was not a total success: Michael complained of difficulty in breathing and so he was referred to Dr. Steven Hoefflin, who performed a second operation. Hoefflin would become Michael's regular plastic surgeon and this was just the start of many, many more operations to come. At the time, though, no one realised quite where this was going to lead, and Michael was delighted with his new nose, which was slightly smaller than the original. His father had always taunted him about his big nose: well, now it wasn't so big anymore. A very dangerous precedent had been set.

Other problems were beginning to surface, not least Michael's relationship with food. Over the years, all sorts of myths have been perpetuated about how he deliberately kept his weight down so that his voice would retain a childlike quality. The truth is that anyone so obsessed with his appearance would never have a straightforward relationship with food. He admitted as much to Jesse Jackson in their radio interview. 'Well, I've never been a great eater – to tell a little secret, I hate to tell it, I've never been a great eater or a great admirer of food,' he said. 'Even though I appreciate food and the gift of food and how God has given us food to eat, my mother has always had a hard time with me, all my life, forcing me to eat.

'Elizabeth Taylor used to feed me, hand feed me at times, because I do have a problem with eating, but I do my very best and I am eating. Yes, I *am*! So I don't... Please, I don't want anyone to think I'm starving: I am not.'

Decades after the event, it came out that Michael's weight plummeted during times of extreme stress. Throughout his life, he remained very slim, sometimes dangerously so. Just before his death, fans who saw him preparing for his O2 Arena dates reported that his frame was skeletal.

Michael's preoccupation with his career had become overwhelming, but there was a further schism in the family at that point, this time caused by his father. For once, this wasn't directly about Michael, but given his relationship with his mother, it wounded him to the core. In 1973, Joe had had an affair with a woman some 20 years his junior, with whom he had also had a child.

He now admitted the relationship, and the child, to the rest of the family. Michael was utterly appalled and had nothing to do with his father for several years after that. Indeed, the whole family was shaken to the core. Many years later, Janet Jackson gave an interview to *Parade* magazine, talking about her mother Katherine: 'It's a very cold world, and to have gone through what she has had to experience, from having polio as a child to those things with my brother Michael, and then for my father to have had another child,' she said. 'I've been cheated on a lot – I know what that feels like and how that hurts the heart. But I mean, to give us a half-sister, I can't even fathom what that's like for a mother. For her to stay with my father all those years and never abandon her kids, that's true love.'

At the same time, Michael's own sense of isolation was ever deepening. 'Even at home I'm lonely,' he admitted.

'I sit in my room sometimes and cry. It's so hard to make friends – I sometimes walk around the neighbourhood at night, just hoping to find someone to talk to. But I just end up coming home.' And this from a man now well on his way to becoming one of the most successful artists on the planet.

A further single, 'Girlfriend', was released from *Off The Wall*, although in this case only in the UK, where it performed respectably, staying in the Top 50 for five weeks, after which Michael returned to the fold, as it were, to record *Triumph* with his brothers. Along with the rest of the family he was interviewed by journalist Sylvia Chase for the TV programme *20/20*, during which Chase pointed out that although Michael was now 21, he still managed to retain his childlike voice. It was the first time this had ever been commented on. Michael would somehow stop developing and remain forever rooted in the past. In fact, it was a very revealing interview, in which Michael's mother remarked that she was beginning to sense some changes in her son.

'Michael's quiet now,' said Katherine. 'When he was younger, he wasn't that quiet. But I don't know, I think the stage might have done that to him because wherever he goes, everyone's coming up to see Michael Jackson. You know, wanting to see what he looks like, and he said he feels like an animal in a cage.'

Sylvia asked Michael if that was really the case. 'I do

all the time,' was his reply. 'I shouldn't say all the time, but I get embarrassed easily. The most comfortable [place is] on stage, than any place in the world. Being around everyday people, I feel strange.'

The footage was mingled with other members of the family talking. Marlon reminisced that the act really started the day their TV broke down: when it took a long time to be repaired, the family started singing Country & Western to keep themselves amused. Joe Jackson was interviewed, too.

'They resented it,' he said (of the way he got his sons to perform), before talking about the cost of the guitars and the drums, and how the family toured around in their van in the very early days.

They certainly did bear a grudge. In the interview, Michael comes across as charming, if a little diffident, until the subject of those childhood days comes up: the way he talks about the constant rehearsing, and how none of them were ever allowed to go out and play betokens a deep well of bitterness never before hinted at. In other ways, though, the brothers cheerfully admit they were perfectly happy when Michael got all the attention because he was their lead singer. They put him at the front, they said, because of his energy and indeed, that energy fizzed away on stage as strongly as ever.

But again, that sense of Michael's isolation continued to come through. Sylvia Chase put it to him that he had never had to deal with real world. 'That's true in one way, but it's hard to in my position,' said Michael, and he was utterly justified in saying that. 'I try to sometimes, but people won't deal with me in that way, if they see me differently. They won't talk to me as if I were their next-door neighbour.'

Knowing what was to happen to Michael in his later years, there is almost an unbearable poignancy in what came next. Michael had no private life to speak of – he never had done – but in public, it was a different matter altogether. His home was in front of an audience: it was where he was happiest, where he felt he belonged. 'On stage for me is the greatest place in the world,' he said. 'You just light up on stage, it's magic!' 'Do you want to stop?' he was asked. 'No way!' he cried. 'Don't stop till you get enough. I think [the thing] I like most about being on stage is making people happy. I feel I'm here on earth for a reason; I think it's my job to do that. I've been doing it for so long. If the people enjoy it, I'll be happy.'

They certainly enjoyed it back then – and indeed, throughout his career, his fans never stopped enjoying watching him perform. The family was out on the road once more, with one massive sell-out concert after another. On stage Michael always the focal point, the centre of attention. All it needed was one trademark shriek and the fans were beside themselves, screaming the house down, anything to get a piece of the handsome young African American going through the most extraordinary dance moves. Michael's charm, bucketloads of it, was massively in evidence. Meanwhile, his erstwhile rival Donny Osmond languished, forgotten for now in the shadows. Michael was turning into the biggest star the world had ever seen.

Indeed, across the Atlantic the only person who really rivalled Michael Jackson throughout the 1980s was just shyly slipping into the limelight. The then Lady Diana Spencer, with whom he was to become friends, would attract equal attention and, like Michael, this would destroy her in the end. No one else, not even the other two great eighties pop icons Madonna and Prince could come close to the adulation and attention that Michael was to enjoy.

But, as he himself pointed out, he'd been doing it since he was barely out of nappies, and so not only did he have no idea how to lead any other sort of life, nor did he or anyone else envisage the dangers that lay ahead. Back then it was a joy to be alive, either as a member of The Jacksons, or one of their fans. The records were there for the breaking. On 9 July 1981, The Jacksons started the Triumph tour, promoting their latest album in a 39-city tour across the US. No expense was spared, and they even enlisted the services of the magician Dug Henning to lay on their biggest spectacle yet.

Again, the fans were beside themselves as the band broke stadium records, grossed about $5.5 million (a massive sum in those days), played to about 600,000 fans, raised $100,000 for the Atlanta Children's Foundation and ended up recording the Madison Square Garden Concert. It was released as an album, *The Jacksons Live! 1981*. Finally, they completed the tour in the September, with sell-out shows at the Los Angeles Forum, breaking more records still. But this was nothing compared to what was to come: Michael's relationship with Quincy Jones was still in its earliest stages. Between the two of them, they were about to create the most extraordinary, and successful, album of all time.

CHAPTER FIVE

THE GREATEST ALBUM EVER MADE

The year was 1981 and werewolves were all the rage. No less than three werewolf films were released that year, two of which, *The Howling* and *Wolfen*, have largely been forgotten. However, the third achieved status as one of the all-time classic horror movies, albeit with a comic twist: *An American Werewolf in London*. Starring David Naughton and Griffin Dunne as two hapless American tourists, who venture out on the Yorkshire Moors and find considerably more than they bargained for, *American Werewolf* became an absolute sensation, not least because of the groundbreaking special effects, in which a man turned into a wolf. It gained millions of fans worldwide, and one member of the audience was Michael Jackson.

At the time, Michael was casting around for his next

project. By anyone's reckoning, *Off The Wall* had been a massive success: he alone seemed unable to appreciate quite how well it had done, and wanted something bigger, better, groundbreaking, record-shattering – in short, utterly thrilling. Watching *An American Werewolf in London*, an idea began to take shape.

The original film, which was to inspire both the greatest album and the greatest pop video ever made, was a modern take on an ancient tale: that of a man attacked by a supernatural being, who then turns into a monster, himself. David (David Naughton) and Jack (Griffin Dunne) are backpacking around Europe when they drop into a pub, the Slaughtered Lamb (that name alone should have been enough warning that something odd was afoot). The locals warn them not to go out on the Moors at night. However, they choose to ignore them and do just that.

There, they are attacked by an animal that kills Jack and wounds David, although he's so badly injured that he doesn't come round in hospital for another three weeks. When he finally regains consciousness, Jack's ghost, in a distressingly decomposing state, pays a visit to tell David that they were attacked by a werewolf and that he himself has become one. In fact, the only way to avoid further tragedy is for David to kill himself before the next full moon, advice he duly ignores.

After moving in with Nurse Alex (Jenny Agutter),

David turns into a werewolf on the advent of the next full moon and runs amok in London, killing six people. Eventually, he comes round to consciousness with no memory of what happened, mysteriously, in the wolf cage at the Zoo, where the other wolves have wisely left him alone. Looking more decomposed than ever, Jack returns, this time bringing with him the six victims that David slaughtered, who urge him to do the decent thing and take his own life. As night falls, they are still arguing the point, at which stage David returns to wolf-state and thus commences another killing spree. This ends when Alex tells him she loves him. The police then shoot David, returning him – in death – to human form.

Of course, it was a take on a story that had been told so many times, but somehow it fitted in with the spirit of the age. For a start, there was a wicked sense of humour running throughout the movie. The credits congratulate Prince Charles and Lady Diana Spencer on their marriage (given the outcome of that union, it is perhaps fitting that the film was a horror story), while at the same time containing the disclaimer, 'any resemblance to any persons living, dead or undead is coincidental'. *American Werewolf* was produced by Lycanthrope Production, a lycanthrope being another name for a werewolf, while the soundtrack is very lunar influenced: Bobby Darin's 'Blue Moon' is heard over the opening credits, David and Alex make love to Van

Morrison's 'Moondance' and Creedence Clearwater Revival's 'Bad Moon Rising' strums away in the background as David starts to turn into a wolf. A couple of other versions of 'Blue Moon' also feature throughout the film.

What really was the most groundbreaking aspect of it all, however, was the make-up and special effects. It might not look much to the modern, jaundiced eye, but at the time audiences had never seen anything like it. The prosthetics, fake body parts and all-round gore, both in the scenes in which David transforms into a werewolf and when Jack returns, looking increasingly gruesome, were such a hit that the Academy of Motion Picture Arts and Sciences (AMPAS) actually created a new Oscar in honour of them: Outstanding Achievement in Makeup. To a man like Michael, immersed in the world of show business since he was an infant, this was truly, revelatory, groundbreaking stuff.

Then there was the director, John Landis. Years earlier, Landis came up with the idea for the movie when he was working on the film *Kelly's Heroes* as a production assistant in former Yugoslavia. There, he was witness to a gypsy burial ceremony, in which rituals were said over the deceased to prevent him rising from the grave. He wrote the script in 1969 and then abandoned it for a whole decade, going on to gain experience directing such diverse works as *The Kentucky Fried Movie*, National

Lampoon's *Animal House* and *The Blues Brothers*. All were comedies, which is how he managed to infuse the unexpected humour into *American Werewolf* – although this caused problems in acquiring the funding, in that some potential investors considered it too funny to be a horror film and too frightening to be a comedy. Naturally, they were proved wrong.

Reviews, when the film came out, were sensational. 'Carnivorous lunar activities rarely come any more entertaining than this,' wrote Kim Newman in *Empire* magazine. 'A clever mixture of comedy and horror, which succeeds in being both funny and scary,' stated *Variety*, who continued, '*An American Werewolf in London* possesses an overriding eagerness to please that prevents it from becoming off-putting, and special effects freaks get more than their money's worth.' Meanwhile, 'One of the all-time great horror movies, a pitch-perfect mix of belly laughs and genuine scares,' opined Rob Gonsalves at eFilmCritic.com. And, noting that even the Academy Awards had been inspired to something new: 'Director John Landis brings humor to this offbeat reworking of the familiar tale for which Rick Baker received a well deserved Oscar for his make-up (in the first year of that category),' was Emanuel Levy's take.

So, there it was: the Movie of the Moment, the Director of the Moment and the Man of the Moment:

Michael. The union of all three was to produce the most spectacularly successful album ever made to this day; likewise, the accompanying video would change the face of pop culture.

Michael would also record 'Someone In The Dark' from director Steven Spielberg's *E.T.: the Extra-Terrestrial* (1982), which won him a Grammy for Best Album for Children. Afterwards, he himself would forever be associated with E.T., a strange, gentle and childlike figure whose greatest desire was to return home. In Michael's case, of course, home was the childhood that he lost and, despite a lifetime's searching, would never be able to return to again. But now, it was time for what would be the defining moment of his life.

Michael returned to the studios with the same team who made *Off The Wall* and this time, producer Quincy Jones was especially determined to come up with something the likes of which had never been seen before. From the outset, he recognised that this would be an extraordinary hit. 'I knew from the first time I heard it in the studio, because the hair stood straight up on my arms,' he recalled. 'That's a sure sign, and it's never once been wrong. All the brilliance that had been building inside Michael Jackson for 25 years just erupted. It's like he was suddenly transformed from this gifted young man into a dangerous, predatory animal. I'd known Michael since he was 12 years old, but it was like seeing and hearing him for the first time. I was electrified, and so was everybody else involved in the project. That energy was contagious, and we had it cranked so high one night that the speakers in the studio actually overloaded and burst into flames. First time I ever saw anything like that in 40 years in the business. And that's just what the album did when it hit the charts. Biggest-selling album in the history of music hyped by the biggest-selling video of all time – a 14-minute film that had the impact of a hit movie, there's never been anything like it.'

By the time *Thriller* came about, Michael was in a much stronger position, creatively and in every other way, than ever before. For a start, John Branca had negotiated the highest royalties rate ever seen in the business: 37 per cent, or $2 an album. Given the album would go on to sell over 100 million copies, the success of *Thriller* was to make him richer than Croesus. This time, he contributed even more of the music: of the nine tracks that were to end up on the album, Michael wrote four of them: 'Wanna Be Startin' Somethin'', 'The Girl Is Mine' (with Paul McCartney), 'Beat It' and 'Billie Jean' (considered by some to be the best pop song ever written).

Indeed, 'Billie Jean' was based on experience. Michael was used to being mobbed everywhere he went, but in one case, a fan actually managed to get into his back garden. With hindsight, given that it could be the case that Michael's three children are not biologically his, the idea of him fathering an illegitimate child seems a little unlikely, but at the time it was a reflection of what his life had become like.

'Michael wrote "Billie Jean" – and that stuff, you know, it was just highly, highly personal,' Quincy later recalled. 'According to him, he said it was about a girl who climbed over [his] wall and he woke up one morning and she was laying out by the pool, lounging, hanging out with the shades on, bathing suit on... and Michael said she had accused him of being the father of one of her twins. And Michael, on "Billie Jean", he had an intro you could shave on, it was so long. I said, "It's too long, we gotta get to the melody quicker." He said, "But that's the jelly! That's what makes me wanna dance." Now, when Michael Jackson tells you that's what makes him want to dance, the rest of us had to shut up.'

Between April and November 1982 recording took place at the Westlake Recording Studios in Los Angeles. In interviews afterwards, Michael and Quincy recalled a period of an almost insane amount of work, putting in at least 18 hours a day, sleeping on the sofa, and adding the finishing touches to the *E.T.* storybook at the same time.

'The drama surrounding *Thriller* seemed to never end,'

Quincy wrote in the *Los Angeles Times* after Michael's death. 'As we were recording the album, Steven Spielberg asked me to do a storybook song with Michael for *E.T.* We were already behind schedule on *Thriller*, but great, no problem. The movie was a big hit, we loved Steven, and so, off to work we went, with Rod Temperton and Marilyn and Alan Bergman writing the song. Naturally, of course, this would evolve into Steven wanting us to do an *E.T.* album.'

Not only was the workload enormous, but expectations were incredibly high. For a start, Michael was determined to outdo the success of *Off The Wall*. Also, the record industry was by then looking at him through new eyes and it, too, wanted to see what he could come up with. And finally, the music business itself was down in the dumps: not only would a really huge hit would have a massive effect on Michael's career, but it would actually do something for the industry as a whole. Everyone involved knew that, too.

'When we started *Thriller*, the first day at Westlake, we were all there and Quincy walked in, followed by me and Michael and Rod Temperton, and some of the other people,' Bruce Swedien, engineer on the album and a long-term collaborator with Quincy, later recalled. 'Quincy turned to us and he said, "OK, guys, we're here to save the recording industry." Now that's a pretty big responsibility, but he meant it. And that's why those albums, and especially *Thriller*, sound so incredible. The basic thing is, everybody who was involved gave 150 per cent... Quincy's like a director of a movie and I'm like a director of photography, and it's Quincy's job to cast [it]. Quincy can find the people and he gives us the inspiration to do what we do.' And they certainly did what they did in the recording studios, back then.

There was also the title track itself, written by Rod Temperton. Michael had, in the past, done the spoken lead into a number of his songs, but this time round it was felt it would be best performed by an actor. And who better than one of the best-known horror movie actors of them all?

'When I wrote "Thriller", I'd always envisioned this talking section at the end and didn't really know what we were going to do with it,' recalled Rod Temperton. 'But one thing I'd thought about was to have somebody, a famous voice, in the horror genre, to do this vocal. Quincy's [then] wife [Peggy Lipton] knew Vincent Price, so Quincy said to me, "How about if we got Vincent Price?" And I said, "Wow, that'd be amazing if we could get him..."'

And so they got him, and the rest was musical history, although there were still a few mountains to climb. For a start, after the gruelling recording schedule experienced by the team, the final version of the album was not deemed up to scratch. 'It sounded... terrible,' wrote Quincy Jones in the *LA Times*. 'After all of that great work we were doing, it wasn't there. There was total silence in the studio, and one by one we walked across the hall for some alone time. We'd put too much material on the record. Michael was in tears. We took two days off, and in the next eight days, we set about reshaping the album, mixing just one song a day. Rod cut a verse from "The Lady in My Life" and we shortened the long, long intro to "Billie Jean", something Michael hated to do because he said the intro "made him want to dance." And then, finally, they were ready to go.'

Somewhat inexplicably, the first single from the album, released in October 1982, was also one of the weakest tracks on it: 'The Girl Is Mine'. Michael had recorded with Paul McCartney before, most notably 'Say Say Say' and 'The Man', but although the song performed very respectably, reaching No. 2 on the Billboard Hot 100, No. 1 on the R&B Singles Chart and No. 8 in the UK, eventually going platinum after selling 1.3 million copies, the critics were not inspired. They felt that Michael and Quincy were betraying their African American heritage by creating music for white people, and this in turn considerably dampened down expectations for *Thriller*, the album. If that's what it's going to be made up of, went the reasoning then Michael Jackson would not be making much of an impact with this one at all.

Thriller, the album, was released in November 1982 to generally positive reviews, although it would still be some little while before it turned into the phenomenon it became. Christopher Connelly in *Rolling Stone* described it as, 'a zesty LP, whose up-tempo workouts don't obscure its harrowing dark message', although he didn't like the title track, calling it 'silly camp', and appeared not to understand why Vincent Price was on board.

The New York Times rated it as well, especially 'Human Nature', which it described as, 'a haunting, brooding ballad by Steve Porcaro and John Bettis, with an irresistible chorus and it should be an enormous hit.' Adding, 'there are other hits here, too, lots of them. Best of all, with a pervasive confidence infusing the album as a whole, *Thriller* suggests that Mr. Jackson's evolution as an artist is far from finished.'

Self-proclaimed 'Dean of American rock critics' Robert Christgau was another fan, calling it, 'almost classic'. 'Beat It', he liked – 'the triumph and the thriller', but 'The Girl is Mine' less so – 'Michael's worst idea since "Ben."' There were one or two negative voices, such as Paolo Hewitt in *Melody Maker*: 'This is not a good LP.' The album itself was deemed 'bland', while, 'Jackson seems to have lost his talent for turning gross into gold.' History was not on Paolo's side, but at the time, while *Thriller* was selling perfectly respectably, it had yet to take off into the stratosphere.

And then, in January 1983, 'Billie Jean' became the second single from the album. It was a sensation, topping both the US and UK charts: ironically, this was Quincy's least favourite track. He didn't even like the title, believing people would think it related to the Grand Slam tennis player, Billie Jean King. It was also a highly controversial track: Michael had, himself, been the subject of a somewhat unlikely paternity suit, on top of which the newspapers were full of stories that his parents might be separating, in the wake of the news of Joe's love child. There was a dark aspect to it, a paranoia not normally associated with the sunny-natured star. Yet it was this song that defined Michael Jackson as *the* star of the era: if the transformation had begun with *Off The Wall*, then it was complete with 'Billie Jean'. Life had never been normal for Michael, but after this, there truly was no turning back.

Although *Thriller* is probably the most famous video from the album, if not of all time, a video accompanied 'Billie Jean', too. It was a sensational achievement: Michael dressed up as a song and dance man, prowling down the pavement, each paving slab lighting up as he stepped on it. Although *Thriller* was to change MTV's stance on rock music, 'Billie Jean' did receive some airplay on the channel, too. According to many, that was what made it quite the cultural sensation it became: people could sing like Michael or they could dance like

Michael, but no one else could do both. Add to that the professionalism, the determination and the sheer skill and talent involved.

'Though it may not sound like it today, "Billie Jean" is one of the most revolutionary songs in the history of popular music,' Joe Queenan wrote in the *Guardian*. "Billie Jean" was groundbreaking because it introduced the idea that a single must be accompanied by a high-production video – preferably by someone who is a bit of a hoofer – thereby transforming a run-of-the-mill song release into an "event". "Billie Jean's" greatest importance is that it launched the Michael Jackson era, a period in which the entire population of the planet made a group decision to follow the career of one star, and one star only. This was an era in which a fabulously gifted performer like Prince was forced into a distant second-fiddle role, because even though Prince could dance, he couldn't dance like Michael Jackson.'

Momentum began to gather around the album. It was now that Michael made the groundbreaking appearance at the Motown 25: Yesterday, Today, Forever ceremony, and even that almost didn't come about. 'Suzanne de Passe had called me,' said Don Mischer, producer of the show, in an interview for the Archive of American Television (AAT). 'She was a longtime associate of Berry Gordy and Motown Records, and we started having meetings about doing a celebratory show about the 25th anniversary of Motown… It was a tough show to do. Suzanne was so eloquent in talking to them. Our approach was this is the 25th anniversary of Motown, it's a celebration of music that started in Detroit and has now swept the nation. It did so much for civil rights, for the merging of black and white music. "You must do your most famous Motown song. You can't do a new song," we said that to Marvin Gaye and to The Tops and The Temps, and everybody else who was on that show.'

However, that was not exactly what Michael wanted to do and so a compromise had to be reached. 'We wanted to bring the Jackson 5 back together,' continued Don. 'Michael Jackson said, "I will consider coming back again with my brothers, but I want to do a new song." Suzanne and I said, "Look, we can't do that. If you say no to Marvin Gaye and no to Lionel Ritchie, no to a new song, how are you going to say yes, to Michael Jackson? We really, really can't do this. It's not fair, it's got to be favored nations, everybody's got to do the traditional stuff."'

Not for the first time, Michael got his way. The stakes were extremely high, and to have the person who was the hottest name in show business, combined with the brothers with whom he'd started out, was just too good an opportunity to miss out on. But, as with all truly great show-business anecdotes, everything was left to the very last second to clear up. 'It was like the Monday before the show, which was being shot on a Friday, that we finally realised that it was too much to lose not to have the Jackson 5 reunite on the 25th anniversary of Motown,' said Don. 'So we said, we're going to at least have to consider it. It's now the night before the Friday night taping; I'm in the truck. Michael shows up. We talk about how we're going to do the Jackson 5. Michael always gives me hand cues about when to do certain things: "When I break my wrist, I do this; when I point this way, I take my hat off, and we, you know, whatever."'

Meanwhile, the performers and audience were all A-list, nothing had been entirely clarified and there was a real chance something could go horribly, badly wrong. 'So, Linda Ronstadt's out there, Smokey's out there, Diana Ross was just sitting in the audience, a bunch of runners and Passe sitting around,' he went on. 'And Michael says, "OK, now let's try the new song." Michael starts to do "Billie Jean" with the moonwalk, and I kick myself today: why didn't I pop a piece of tape into a tape recorder in the truck and shoot this? I didn't think about it. It was just another song we were prepared not to use. And man, it just electrified everyone! You know the rest of the story. He ended up doing it and it became one of the real remarkable moments in television. I shudder to think how close we came to not having that moment ever happen.'

That was, in fact, the moment when Michael debuted

the moonwalk to the rest of the world. It was to become his signature, his trademark, and a part of his act guaranteed to send audiences into a frenzy of excitement. Michael, however, was always very generous about where it came from: he did not invent it himself, he told Jesse Jackson, but it was something he picked up from watching children on the street.

'The moonwalk is a dance,' he said. 'I would love to take credit for it, but I can't because I have to be completely honest here. These black children in the ghettos are... they have the most phenomenal rhythm of anybody on the Earth. I'm not joking. I learned; I get a lot of ideas from watching these black children. They have perfect rhythm. From just riding through Harlem, I remember in the early, you know, late seventies, early eighties, I would see these kids dancing on the street and I would see these kids doing these sliding backwards, kind of like an illusion dancing, I call it. I took a mental picture of it, a mental movie of it. I went into my room upstairs in Encino, and I would just start doing the dance, and create and perfect it. But it definitely started within the black culture, no doubt. That's where it comes from.'

It was an absolute sensation and, for the moonwalk alone, Michael earned his place in the history books. But more, far more, was to come. The release of the album's title track was fast approaching and he was already planning his next move on a scale simply never before envisaged.

Billie Jean had been one of the most innovative videos ever made, but now Michael wanted to go one better. By this time, he had film experience himself and he had not forgotten *An American Werewolf In London*, so he decided to cut to the chase. Michael wanted to be a werewolf, and so he went straight to the man who could make him one: director of *American Werewolf*, John Landis.

Although already a well-established director, in making what was to be the most groundbreaking pop video ever put together, Landis would become a part of pop-music history as well. He recalled the experience with affection: '*Thriller*, the album, had been in the Top 10 for a year, and maybe No. 1 for most of that year, but now it was going down – but still, in the Top 10 after a year.

'There had been two videos made, *Billie Jean* and *Beat It*, and both of those had been very successful. Michael saw *An American Werewolf in London*, and he contacted me and asked me if I would make a video with him. And I said, "No, actually – because they were basically commercials, right?" But he persisted and said, "No, no, no – I really wanna make it." So, when I returned to LA, I called Rick Baker, who had done the make-up effects for *American Werewolf*, and said, "Rick, Michael Jackson wants to become a monster."'

Quite simply, nothing like this had ever been done before. Even Michael's video for 'Billie Jean', hailed as revolutionary from all sides, was unable to top it. For the video for 'Thriller' was to be nothing less than a mini-film: a story within a story, within a story, that saw Michael take on several roles, from doting boyfriend to zombie, to werewolf to himself. It was an extraordinary event, and although he had others involved to bring his vision to reality, *Thriller* was above all his creation, a work that was to change the face of popular entertainment.

For a start, the budget was on a scale totally different from any pop video before. '*Thriller* cost about $600,000, which at the time was huge because the average rock video cost between $50,000 and $100,000, and we made one for $600,000,' recalled John Landis in an interview for the website Fangoria.com. 'But it cost $600,000 for a lot of reasons. For instance, the average rock video was just the length of the song, 3 minutes. And you just played the song and people lip-synced to it. *Thriller* was a theatrical short. It was two reels, so it was 14 minutes long. We had union make-up artists, union dancers, plus I took the original song "Thriller" – the original tracks, which was like, a 38-track song, and broke it down and re-cut it to be almost like 12 minutes long. And then Elmer Bernstein wrote music, and then we did a theatrical mix.'

Right from the start, everyone knew they were involved in something amazing. 'So, *Thriller*, it's not really fair to compare it to the other videos from the time because we were so much more ambitious,' Landis continued. 'We were "making a little movie", that was our whole approach. Plus, it was intended to be a theatrical short. It played with *Fantasia* in Los Angeles, and again when you ask, "How did it happen?" – that was a total accident, that was a vanity video. Michael Jackson had made *Billie Jean* and *Beat It* – those two videos were hugely successful, directed by Bob Giraldi – and *Thriller* the album was the No. 1 album and the biggest-selling album of all-time for over a year. It had dropped down to No. 6, and it was over essentially, and it was on its way down.'

In fact, it proved the final impetus for Michael. He had succeeded beyond his wildest dreams in creating, along with Quincy and the rest of the crew, the most astonishing album ever made, but it was the fact that *Thriller* was slowly, inevitably, yielding its pole position that spurred him to ever-greater heights.

'So he called me, and he had seen *An American Werewolf in London* and he wanted to turn into a monster,' Landis went on. 'That was his contribution, he wanted to morph... So, going in, CBS Records... wouldn't give us any money because they just assumed this was on its way down, and "Why throw good money at it?" because it wasn't going to make them any more money. But Michael wanted to do it, so he was gonna put up the money and I said, "Don't put up your own money, that's wrong" and it was George Folsey who suggested that we shoot us shooting it.'

Indeed, that experience was to prove groundbreaking too. Michael didn't just put together a phenomenally successful video; he released a documentary on the back of it, detailing how it was made. All this just added to the mystique: nothing like it had ever been done before and the public just couldn't get enough of it.

However, once the video was made, another problem raised its head. MTV hardly showed videos released by black artists. *Thriller* was to change all that, too. 'Until *Thriller*, MTV had simply refused to play videos from black artists,' recalled Walter Yetnikoff, former head of CBS Records. 'They said their audience wasn't ready for them. But *Billie Jean* and *Beat It* – both from *Thriller* – were simply too good to be ignored. MTV finally gave in and now they're playing all kinds of music. I'm certain it was Michael who broke that colour barrier.'

In actual fact, it was even more dramatic than that. Incandescent with rage at the way his major star was being treated, Yetnikoff quite simply threatened to withhold his artists from appearing on MTV unless Michael Jackson was given a decent amount of airplay.

His tactic worked. MTV began playing the video of *Thriller* and increasingly, it became apparent that here was a hit like nothing before.

In the video, Michael starts off by playing a handsome guy out on a date, taking his girl to the movies. It's a horror film, but she can't bear it and insists they leave. Having done so, Michael (looking sensational in an orange leather outfit) prances around her, singing and dancing about the Thriller. But, as they go deeper into the woods, he too begins to change. He turns into a zombie. At this point the two, having conveniently arrived in a graveyard, watch as headstones start to move. Soon the scene is full of the undead. And then they begin one of the most famous sequences in modern dance history, the zombies in the graveyard, before Michael finally goes the whole hog and turns into a wolf himself.

'Everyone involved knew that nothing like this had ever been done before, and so they needed a new way to introduce it to the world, too,' said John Landis. 'Videos didn't get premières, but films did, and this was a film – and so why not? And so, in due course a première of the film-ette was held, another tremendous success.

'We had a première – which was a riot – because Michael wanted a première,' he went on. 'I've been to the Oscars and I've been to the Baftas, I've been to the Emmys; I've been to the Golden Globes, and I've never been anywhere like this première. It was incredible. There was everyone from Diana Ross and Warren Beatty to Prince. It was nuts. Amazing... got a standing ovation and all that stuff, and they're shouting, "Encore, encore," and I said, "Encore? There is no fucking encore!" Then Eddie Murphy got up and shouted, "Show the goddamn thing again!" So they sat and they watched *Thriller* again. Why not? It was just amazing, it was just amazing...'

But that wasn't the end of the story. Michael and his team were shattering records, breaking ground and simply astonishing everyone with their creativity. Their commercial nous was quite something, too. In an unprecedented move, the short film of *Thriller* was followed by a slightly longer documentary: *The Making Of Thriller*. It was a little padded out, perhaps, but yet another triumph that also made a contribution to the then nascent cable TV industry.

'That *Making of Thriller* was 45 minutes long, and the video was 15 minutes long, so together it's an hour. So we can sell it, and we sold it to Showtime,' John Landis recalled. 'It was one of the first cable TV events. MTV went insane when we sold it to Showtime. They said, "How can you do that to us?" and we said, "OK, you want it? Buy it!" So they paid some money, and we got money from Showtime and MTV, and that's how we financed it. We used to call *The Making of Thriller*, *The*

Making of Filler because it had to be 45 minutes, that's why everything is in it. I owned *Werewolf* so there's pieces of *Werewolf*. He [Michael] owned "Can You Feel It?" so we put "Can You Feel It?", everything we could throw in there. Home movies? We put them in there!

'It turned out very well, but it was nobody's plan. It did a lot of things. *The Making Of Thriller* created the whole "making of" business, which is now a business. The biggest impact *Thriller* had was that the record went back to No. 1 – that was a big deal and showed the huge influence that these things could have internationally.'

Yet another development on the back of all this concerned home entertainment itself: 'A guy named Austin Furst, who had a company called Vestron Video, called me and said, "I'd like to release *Thriller* and *The Making Of Thriller* as a home video," and I said, "Yeah, but it's airing for free on television,"' Landis continued. 'This was at the time when home videos cost $80–$90, and the creation of things like Blockbuster and Mom & Pop Video Stores came about because to buy a movie then was $80–$90 bucks, so no one would buy them, but they'd rent them. So, selling these things, they'd be sold to stores to rent and that's why they were so expensive.

'And he came up with the idea – Austin told me the term and it was the first time I'd ever heard it – to "Sell-through". So, it was low-budget, $19.95, which was enough that you could actually buy it. That then went out and sold over a million copies, which at the time was huge!'

Of course Landis had worked with some of the biggest names in the business, but even he was taken aback at what being around Michael Jackson entailed. All major stars are subject to hysterical behaviour from fans, but this was something else. By now, Michael had risen above pop superstardom to become the icon, the symbol, of the age. 'When we made *Thriller*, working with Michael was like The Beatles,' he revealed. 'You know, when John Lennon said that thing about "We're more popular than Christ", I totally understand what he was talking about because being with Michael at that moment was incredible. People would see him and they would faint, or women would have orgasms – I'm not kidding, people would be overcome.

'It was amazing, the only time in my entire life when I've ever been truly terrified. It sounds funny, but you're rarely scared in your life, and the only time I was really terrified... Right after *Thriller* came out, Michael and my wife, and baby daughter... we went to Disney World in Florida, and I have this picture in my library of Michael and I and Mickey Mouse – and we went to take this picture by the castle, and there was this lawn that was about 20 x 20 foot and had this little rope chain around it like a bank, and the photographer was there, and Michael and I and Mickey came through these underground tunnels where you come "up" and within minutes there were 5,000 people there around us. They were screaming and I thought they're going to eat us.

'I was just terrified, and Mickey was like, "Get me outta here!" We were scared to death, and it was like, "Oh my God, someone is going to die!" And Michael was just like, "Hi, how are you?" and it didn't phase him at all. Miraculously, this Cadillac limousine just appeared out of nowhere, and I still don't know where it came from. They took us and threw us in there, and then the people went on the car – it was really scary.

'I find it interesting, as I've worked with Paul McCartney and Michael Jackson, and The Blues Brothers and David Bowie, and a lot of people that have gone through that experience and man, I think it's difficult to remain sane under those circumstances. When you see what happened to Elvis – I mean, I understand it, but with that level of stardom, and that level of celebrity, it's a miracle if you can make it through with any sense of sanity after that.'

Of course, Michael was to pay a very heavy price. At the time, though, he'd achieved what he'd said he was going to do: he'd made history, he'd made money and he'd made an album still unequalled to this day. According to *Guinness World Records*, *Thriller* is the world's all-time best-selling album, with sales estimated at 104 million. The album is only one of three to remain in the Top 10 of the Billboard 200 for a full year (the others are *Falling Into You* by Celine Dion and Alanis Morissette's *Jagged Little Pill*). *Thriller* spent 80 consecutive weeks in the Top 10, 37 of which were at No. 1. It is also the first album of only three in history to produce seven Billboard Hot 100 Top Ten singles and the first, and to date only, record to be the best-selling album of two years (1983 and 1984) in the US. Where could Michael possibly go from here?

CHAPTER SIX
DISASTER STRIKES

By early 1984, Michael Jackson towered like a colossus over the world of entertainment, and for the rest of the decade, he would dominate as no artist had ever done before. With *Thriller* breaking records left, right and centre, and while the world looked on in slack-jawed amazement each time he performed the moonwalk, it seemed Michael could do no wrong, as indeed, he couldn't. But a terrible accident was to shatter his already fragile self-image, to make him become even more conscious of his appearance and very nearly ruin his health for good.

Meanwhile, the record industry was treating Michael Jackson as its saviour. Total domestic revenue in the US had risen to $4.1 billion, the best year since 1978, and Michael Jackson's influence was credited for that. 'Star of records, radio, rock video,' gushed normally buttoned-up *Time* magazine. 'A one-man rescue team for the music business. A songwriter who sets the beat for a decade. A dancer with the fanciest feet on the street. A singer who cuts across all boundaries of taste and style and color too.'

In the wake of his Motown appearance, Michael agreed to one last tour with his brothers: the Victory Tour (unusually, there wasn't a tour to support *Thriller*, but it hardly needed one). Many believed this to be an act of generosity towards his brothers, who all stood to benefit financially from the shows, although there was little doubt as to who the audience was really coming to see. As the tour closed, Michael also signed a deal with Pepsi for £7 million, a colossal sum at the time, to become one of a stable of huge stars to advertise the product. This would very nearly prove his undoing.

On 27 January 1984, the accident occurred. In front of an audience of 3,000 fans, Michael was performing 'Billie Jean' when a spectacular fire display erupted behind him. He was showered in sparks and his hair caught fire. In an attempt to control the flames, he whipped off his jacket, while his brothers and other staff on site rushed to help: Michael, meanwhile, remained so calm that some members of the audience actually thought this was all part of the act. 'He was wonderful,' said one, Virginia Watson. 'He reassured people even as he was being taken away on a stretcher.'

Michael was taken to the Brotman Memorial Hospital, while plastic surgeon Steven Hoefflin, who was trained in burns care, rushed to his side. Later, he commented on his patient's condition. 'He is in discomfort,' he said. 'It will take a few weeks to determine the hair loss.' In actual fact, Michael suffered second-degree burns, which scarred his hair follicles and left him with a bald patch. Subsequently, he underwent 80 minutes of laser surgery to repair his scalp. Later in his life, Michael would return to visit the burns unit at the hospital, demonstrating his concern for those suffering from these kinds of terrible injuries. He would also go on to donate his $1.5 million from the Pepsi commercial to the Michael Jackson Burn Center for Children.

The accident marked a turning point in Michael's life. For a start, it made him far more self-conscious about his appearance: shortly after the incident, he would have the third of his nose jobs. From that moment on, his predilection for plastic surgery grew. This was also the start of his addiction to painkillers. And finally, according to his friend, music producer David Gest, who was later to marry – and divorce – Liza Minnelli, his personality changed, too. 'Michael was in so much pain after that, he became unbalanced,' he revealed. 'The trauma and the pills changed him. Before then, he had a tight hold of his career. The accident didn't make

Michael moody or more distant towards me, but he did become a different person.'

Eventually, Michael was awarded $1.5 million by PepsiCo, which he gave to charity, along with the $5 million he was paid for the Victory Tour. And in public, at least, no change was evident. Michael went on to receive eight Grammys for *Thriller* and also travelled to the White House to accept an award from President Reagan for his support for charities that helped overcome alcohol and substance abuse.

But for a man already so conscious of his appearance, the experience must have been devastating. Ironically, at this time 'Michael Jackson' dolls went into production, which meant that at the very moment when the original was fretting that he might be scarred for life, millions of fans were investing in an idealised representation. And indeed, his appearance was becoming more striking. Increasingly, Michael sported some form of military uniform whenever he appeared in public, sometimes stage costumes and at other times, the real thing.

★ ★ ★

At the beginning of 1985 Michael was reunited with his friend and producer Quincy Jones as one of a whole raft of major American celebrities who got together to record the song 'We Are The World'. In the wake of a terrible famine in Ethiopia, a group of British artists, under the wing of Bob Geldof of the Boomtown Rats, had previously recorded the charity hit 'Do They Know It's Christmas?'. However, attempts by Geldof to put together a US version of Band Aid had come to nothing due to scheduling difficulties, after which Harry Belafonte took up the baton. About 45 artists swiftly signed up.

'We Are The World' was written by Michael and Lionel Richie, and produced by Quincy Jones. The 10-hour session at the A&M Recording Studio in Los Angeles was not without incident, however: many of the male stars found that the key was much too high for them and so, at the beginning of the video, either had to mime or just not sing at all. (The chorus was later played in a lower key.) Artists included Stevie Wonder, Kenny Rogers, Tina Turner, Billy Joel, Diana Ross, Bruce Springsteen and others too numerous to mention: it was a remarkably stress-free occasion. 'I did expect to see more ego,' one of the participants, Paul Simon, confessed. 'You know, The Gloved One meets The Boss and things like that, but it's really not. It's really a pleasurable experience, and I think everybody feels the same way.' Ultimately, the extended version of the song ran to over seven minutes, with 21 separate vocal solos.

Given the circumstances surrounding its release, the record would almost certainly have been a sensation, whether or not Michael was involved, but like everything he touched around that time, it promptly went into the stratosphere. 'We Are The World' became the fastest-selling single of the modern pop era: the initial shipment of 800,000 copies sold out within three days of its release on 7 March 1985. It went on to sell 7.5 million and was released on an album of the same name, which included a contribution from Prince and another charity single, 'Tears Are Not Enough'. Ultimately, $63 million was raised for famine relief.

By this time, Michael was beginning to assemble the menagerie that would eventually make up the zoo at Neverland. Alongside Quincy, he appeared in one interview to talk about *Thriller*: wearing a bright blue military outfit and sunglasses, he played with his pet boa constrictor Muscles and confided that he'd always kept boas. 'I love animals,' he went on. It turned out that he was collecting a fair number of them around him: llamas, deer and an ape who was to become famous, Bubbles the chimp.

Born in 1983, in a medical facility in Texas, Bubbles would go everywhere with the singer. Frequently, he was dressed in a smaller version of the same outfit as the singer and developed quite a following himself. In 1985, Michael launched a range of toys called Michael's Pets, with some of the proceeds going to charity. The soft toys, $22 each, included a frog, dog, rabbit, snake, ostrich, giraffe, llama and, of course, Bubbles, as well as

Michael himself, who appeared as a bear, wearing sunglasses and a fedora. It, too, turned to gold. Michael and Bubbles would enjoy a long and enduring relationship, with the tabloids delighting in one bizarre tale after another.

Michael's relationship with Bubbles played very differently with different people. Some saw it as evidence of his childlike nature, taking such delight in a beast of the field; others regarded it as a little too eccentric. The nickname 'Wacko Jacko', which Michael at first found amusing and came to cordially loathe, duly emerged. But most people just found it amusing. Michael taught Bubbles to moonwalk, took him everywhere and once commented, 'My chimp is a constant delight.' There is nothing that odd, after all, in loving animals, and after a childhood deprived of affection, many would see it as understandable that Michael enjoyed this particular bond.

Certainly, the rumours got wilder and wilder. Bubbles was said to have an agent. Bubbles was said to have a bodyguard. Bubbles sat in for the recording of the *Bad* album, along with the snake, Muscles, and Bubbles appeared in the video for 'Liberian Girl'. Bubbles went on tour with Michael, shared a suite with him and in some ways appeared extraordinarily human. The singer Kenny Rogers met Michael and Bubbles in 1986. Afterwards, he recorded the meeting: 'Bubbles was so human it was almost frightening,' he said. 'He would take Christopher [Rogers' son] by the hand, walk over to the refrigerator, open it, take out a banana, and hand it to him. Christopher was amazed... we all were.'

Bubbles was actually only one of a number of chimps that Michael possessed, but he was certainly the most famous, living in the star's private quarters, sleeping in a crib in his bedroom and dining with his owner at the table. It is noteworthy that one of Michael's closest friends, Elizabeth Taylor, understood the attachment: when she opened the Elizabeth Taylor Medical Center in Washington D.C., her escorts were Michael and Bubbles, in matching military uniforms. Both also visited her in Bel-Air.

Of course, it is notable that Michael and Elizabeth were child stars who went on to develop a great love of animals. The world of show business does not contain a great many examples of warmth and generosity, and both would have learned to live with treachery, backstabbing and ruthlessness pretty much as part of the norm. Animals cannot answer back and nor, in most cases, are they likely to turn on you if your record is more successful than theirs. It is not so extraordinary that Bubbles played a big part in Michael's life until he had children of his own.

Nor was it so surprising that Michael and Elizabeth, both figures of global fascination minus a childhood, should become so strongly attached. They met during the *Thriller* days, when Elizabeth asked for tickets to one of his concerts: Michael gave her 14. The tickets were not very good ones, however, and so Elizabeth and her party left. Michael rang her in tears, they started lengthy telephone conversations, and so a friendship developed. The two used to sneak into cinemas together and sit in the back, holding hands.

Writer Paul Theroux spoke to the singer about their friendship and published the results in the *Daily Telegraph* after Michael's death. 'She's a warm, cuddly blanket that I love to snuggle up to and cover myself with,' he said. 'I can confide in her and trust her. In my business, you can't trust anyone… You don't know who's your friend because you're so popular and there's so many people around you. You're isolated, too. Becoming successful means that you become a prisoner. You can't go out and do normal things. People are always looking at what you're doing.'

Theroux asked Michael if he had had that experience himself. 'Oh, lots of times,' was his reply. 'They try to see what you're reading, and all the things you're buying. They want to know everything. There are always paparazzi downstairs. They invade my privacy, they twist reality, they're my nightmare. Elizabeth is someone who loves me, really loves me… But Elizabeth is also like a mother, and more than that: she's a friend. She's Mother Teresa, Princess Diana, the Queen of England and

Wendy. We have great picnics. It's so wonderful to be with her. I can really relax with her because we've lived the same life and experienced the same thing. The great tragedy of childhood stars. We like the same things. Circuses. Amusement parks. Animals.'

Theroux pointed out that both were globally famous, and as such, cut off from the rest of the world. 'It makes people do strange things,' Michael agreed. 'A lot of our famous luminaries become intoxicated because of it – they can't handle it. And your adrenaline is at the zenith of the universe after a concert – you can't sleep. It's maybe two in the morning and you're wide awake. After coming off stage, you're floating.'

Given that, how surprising was it his other great friend happened to be a chimp?

Unfortunately, the advent of the children made it impossible for Bubbles to stay. When Michael's second child, Prince Michael II, was born in 2002, Bubbles started to show aggressive tendencies and was subsequently removed to an animal sanctuary in Sylmar, California, where Michael would visit him with his young family. According to Bob Dunn, who cared for the chimp, this was especially painful for Michael, as he thought of Bubbles as being his first child. 'Bubbles definitely missed him when they parted and will miss him now,' he said, in the wake of the star's death. 'Chimpanzees are intelligent. They remember people and stuff. Bubbles and Michael were close friends and playmates.' Alas, no more.

By this stage, nearing his late twenties, Michael was seriously rich and about to become even more so. Since hiring John Branca to represent him, an arrangement that lasted until Michael's death, he had surrounded himself with a coterie of advisors to build up his fortune even further. Ironically, though, another enormously wealthy pop star gave him one of the best bits of financial advice he ever received.

For some years now, Michael and Paul McCartney had been friends, having worked together and socialised with one another. As two of the most famous performers in the world, they understood the pressure the other was under, too. Both were enormously wealthy, and the frugal Paul, known to be careful with his cash, nonetheless gave his friend a useful piece of advice. Buy music catalogues, he told Michael, the means by which royalties are earned each time a song is played. He himself was earning tens of millions every year from other people's songs.

Michael took him at his word. Shortly after this conversation, Associated Television Corporation's subsidiary, ATV Music, put its music catalogue up for sale. This included Northern Songs, itself a music catalogue that contained several hundred Beatles' numbers, including such classics as 'Yesterday' and 'Let It Be'. Michael acted fast and bid for the catalogue.

Ultimately, the battle to get his hands on this incredibly lucrative stash was successful, but it would take 10 months to come to fruition. At first, Paul McCartney refused to join a bidding war, but then changed his mind and tried to persuade Yoko Ono, John Lennon's widow, to join him. But she couldn't, or wouldn't, and so eventually Michael acquired the catalogue for $47.5 million, a spectacular investment which went on to be worth $450 million, the backbone of a great deal of his wealth.

Sadly, this would put a strain on his relationship with Paul McCartney. 'I think it's dodgy to do things like that,' pronounced Paul at the time. 'To be someone's friend and then buy the rug they're standing on.' For his part, Michael was never repentant: in 2007, when he released the remixed version of 'Thriller' to celebrate the original's 25th birthday, Paul's voice had been taken off the song 'The Girl Is Mine' and replaced with that of Black Eyed Peas rapper Will.I.Am. In a statement issued after Michael's death, though, Sir Paul stated that he and Michael had not fallen out, just drifted apart over the years and that he had happy memories of their time spent working together.

To a public more accustomed to seeing the childlike aspect to Michael, this came as something of a surprise. He was turning out to be an incredibly astute businessman: gentle, shy, maybe – but still very, very sharp. Over time, he would go on to make some other spectacular investments, most notably his Neverland ranch, but this back catalogue not only brought him an income and increased massively in value, it was also a saving grace in later years when his finances were not so sound. Back then, however, it was just a sensationally good deal.

Michael has a 'sound business sense,' remarked his manager, Frank Dileo. 'A lot of artists don't want to know anything about business affairs, but Michael is involved in every facet of his career. He's not one of those people who stops thinking when he walks out of the recording studio or off the stage.' On another occasion, however, he commented that Michael was a strange cross between 'E.T. and Howard Hughes'.

But Michael was more than capable of appreciating his new purchase on an aesthetic level, too. 'The melodies,' he told one interviewer from the *LA Times*. 'They are so lovely and structured so perfectly.' And his favourites were, 'Yesterday', 'Here, There and Everywhere', 'Fool on the Hill', 'Let It Be', 'Hey Jude', 'Eleanor Rigby', 'Penny Lane' and 'Strawberry Fields Forever'.

In 1986, Michael made another excursion into the world of film, this time in a sci-fi production titled *Captain Eo*. Some of Hollywood's biggest names were involved. Directed by Francis Ford Coppola, the executive producer was George Lucas and Anjelica

Huston starred in the role of Supreme Leader. The story had Captain Eo (Michael) leading a space mission to present the Supreme Leader (a wicked queen) with a gift. He flies to her frankly misshapen planet, twisted steel everywhere, with his sidekicks Fuzzball, Idee and Odee, a double-headed pilot (Major Domo), the security officer and Hooter, who resembled an elephant. The crew are captured and threatened with torture, but a couple of them transform into musical instruments, spellbinding the evil queen. Eventually, after more fuss Eo triumphs, transforms the evil one into a great beauty, makes her planet a paradise and departs.

Though only a short film (17 minutes), two new songs were introduced: 'Another Part of Me', which also appeared on the album *Bad*, and 'We Are Here to Change The World'. It was notable for its extraordinary 3-D effects and the fact that it was turned into an attraction at Disneyland, where it could be viewed in all its full 3-D glory. While still doing the rounds of theatres, it was shown with lasers, star fields and smoke effects, making it the most expensive short film ever produced.

Rumours still swirled about Michael's private life, however, and his appearance continued to change. He'd had a fourth nose job, his face was looking softer and less masculine, and now there was a marked cleft in his chin, too. Then, the *National Enquirer* published a photo of him sleeping in an oxygen chamber and this really was a story that would not drop. It was claimed Michael, by now 28, was doing this to prevent himself from ageing. What seems more likely is that he himself had leaked the story to cultivate a sci-fi image in advance of the new movie.

'In the publicist's view, Jackson, as that anecdote suggests, was far from a victim,' commented publicist Bob Jones, who had worked with Michael and, it should be said, had been fired by the star (and might thus have had an axe to grind). 'Instead, he orchestrated the leaks to the press about Jackson's chimpanzee, Bubbles, about the hyperbaric sleeping chamber, about whatever eccentricity that made Michael Jackson, the King of Pop, more interesting, more mysterious.'

Whatever the truth, Michael himself was to grow heartily sick of this story and any others that made him out to be some sort of a freak. 'Why not just tell people I'm an alien from Mars?' he told his biographer J. Randy Taraborrelli in 1984. 'Tell them I eat live chickens and do a voodoo dance at midnight. They'll believe anything you say, because you're a reporter. But if I, Michael Jackson, were to say, "I'm an alien from Mars and I eat live chickens and do a voodoo dance at midnight," people would say, "Oh, man, that Michael Jackson is nuts. He's cracked up. You can't believe a damn word that comes out of his mouth."'

It was an uncharacteristically bitter outburst, although Michael always had a wary attitude towards the media, something that was to emerge in the song 'Scream'. Oprah Winfrey asked him about it, too. 'It's crazy. Why would I want to sleep in a chamber?' asked Michael.

'The rumour was that you were sleeping in the chamber because you didn't want to grow old,' said Oprah.

'That's stupid,' he responded. 'It's completely made up. I'm embarrassed. I'm willing to forgive the press, or forgive anybody. I was taught to love and forgive, which I do have in my heart, [sic] but please don't believe these crazy, horrifying things.'

'Did you buy the Elephant Man's bones?' continued Oprah. 'Were you trying to get them for...'

'No,' said Michael indignantly, stopping the presenter in her tracks. 'That's another stupid story. I love the story of the Elephant Man, he reminds me of me a lot, and I could relate to it; it made me cry because I saw myself in the story, but no, I never asked for the... Where am I going to put some bones? And why would I want some bones? Someone makes it up, and everybody believes it. If you hear a lie often enough, you start to believe it.' Or to put it another way, 'The lie becomes the truth...'

In 1987, the moment the world had been waiting for finally arrived. Unbelievably, it had been nearly five years since the release of *Thriller* and there was intensive speculation as to what Michael Jackson would do next. It caused a problem for him, too. How do you top a success like *Thriller*? The answer is, you can't. Indeed, he couldn't, but nor could anyone else either, which meant that in some ways any new release would always be a comedown.

In some ways, yes, but certainly not in every way, and even taking into account that it didn't match the success of *Thriller*, Michael's next offering, *Bad*, was a superb album and a significant achievement in its own right. It, too, was record breaking: it became the first, and remains to this day, *only* album to feature five Billboard Hot 100 singles. Even when he wasn't breaking his own records, Michael was still streets ahead of the rest.

Although there had appeared to be a long gap between the albums, in actual fact he started work on new material in 1984. Consummate professional that he was, he produced a huge amount to work with. Once again, he teamed up with Quincy Jones, but this time he was given more control than ever. After the success of *Thriller*, who was going to tell Michael Jackson he couldn't pretty much do as he pleased? In the end, it was a 10-track album, with the CD containing a bonus track, 'Leave Me Alone', but there had been plenty more to choose from. Michael had actually recorded 60 new tracks and whittled the selection down to 30 before

Quincy made the final choices. Out of the 11 that made it to the last cut, Michael wrote nine of them.

This was to signal another image change, as well. Michael was still a great fan of military insignia, and never entirely gave it up, but the album's cover, the accompanying video for the title song, the title itself and a great deal else focused on a slightly different Michael from the one who had gone before. Perhaps fed up with the whole 'Wacko Jacko' image, this might have been an attempt to show that he had grown up. For a start, the word 'Bad' in this context meant streetwise, gang-worthy. Michael dressed in leathers for the cover and the accompanying video, which showed him as the leader of a gang dancing their hearts out in the subway. It was a stunning video, one of his best.

The tracks on the album were arranged as follows: 'Bad', 'The Way You Make Me Feel', 'Speed Demon', 'Liberian Girl', 'Just Good Friends' (a duet with Stevie Wonder), 'Part of Me', 'Man In The Mirror', 'I Just Can't Stop Loving You' (another duet, this time with Siedah Garrett), 'Dirty Diana', 'Smooth Criminal' and 'Leave Me Alone'.

To massive expectation, the album was released on 31 August 1987. It debuted at No. 1, the first of Michael's albums to do so, and stayed in pole position for six weeks, selling 8 million copies in the US alone. To this day, it remains his best-selling album in the UK, and to date has sold 30 million copies, placing it behind *Thriller* and *Dangerous* in terms of overall sales. It is also the ninth best-selling album in British chart history.

Bad was to prove Michael's last collaboration with Quincy Jones and there are a couple of footnotes in the making of the album that act as curios to the time it came out. For a start, the title track, 'Bad', was originally planned as a duet between Michael and Prince. The two were perceived to be great rivals and the media coverage would have been enormous. It was Prince himself who shot down that plan, apparently telling Quincy that the song would be a huge hit, whether or not he was involved. A duet between two of the biggest stars of the era would be worth noting to this day, but it was not to be.

Then there was the song 'I Just Can't Stop Loving You'. In the event, the duettist was Siedah Garrett, a well-known artiste, though not quite in Michael's league. The original plan had been to feature someone far more famous: Barbra Streisand, perhaps, or even Whitney Houston. It is thought that both women, along with Aretha Franklin, had been approached. In the event, none of them took up the offer, but the track was still considered to be a great success.

An astonishing nine singles were released from this 11-track disc. It was a mark of quite what outstanding quality Michael was now producing. In the old Jackson

5 days, one or two hits might have been deemed acceptable: now almost the entire album was deemed worthy of standing alone. Between July 1987 and June 1989, they were, in this order: 'I Just Can't Stop Loving You', 'Bad', 'The Way You Make Me Feel', 'Man In The Mirror', 'Dirty Diana', 'Another Part Of Me', 'Smooth Criminal', 'Leave Me Alone' and 'Liberian Girl', the last two released in the UK alone.

Many people in the industry believed that *Bad* was, if anything, better than *Thriller*. The bar had been set unbelievably high, yet Michael still managed to better it. 'Leaving the muddy banks of conjecture – as to sales, as to facial surgery, as to religion, as to is he getting it, and if so, from whom or what? – we can soar into the heart of a nifty piece of work,' wrote Davitt Sigerson in *Rolling Stone* magazine. '*Bad* offers two songs, its title cut and "Man in the Mirror", that stand among the half-dozen best things Jackson has done... *Bad* needs no defense.

'Jackson revives the "Hit The Road Jack" progression and proves (with a lyric beginning with "Your butt is mine" and ending with the answered question, "Who's bad?") that he can out-funk anybody any time. When Jackson declares "the whole world has to answer right now," he is not boasting, but making a statement of fact regarding his extraordinary stardom. If anything, he is scorning the self-coronation of lesser funk royals and inviting his fickle public to spurn him, if it dares. Not since the "Is it good, ya?" of Godfather Brown has a more rhetorical question been posed in funk.'

It was an astonishing achievement, but astonishing achievements simply weren't hacking it any more. Where Michael was concerned, the level of success he was expected to contain just didn't conform to normal standards, and so despite having released probably the best record, both of that year and the surrounding ones, he didn't receive anything like the acclaim of *Thriller*. In fact, *Bad* won just two Grammys: for Best Music Video for 'Leave Me Alone' and Best Engineered Album, a major triumph for most, but not for Michael Jackson. In addition, it was actually voted Worst Single and Worst Album in a poll of 23,000 listeners held by *Rolling Stone*.

Almost certainly this had nothing to do with the music and everything to do with other factors. In some quarters, Michael's eccentricity, Bubbles and oxygen tanks all raised eyebrows, while people began to notice that despite the fact that he was nearing 30, he had still not enjoyed a serious relationship. That last was to become an increasing preoccupation, although Michael still retained a childlike air of innocence which, despite the crotch-grabbing that had now entered his dance routines, served to turn the nay-sayers away.

Besides, he was, in a big way, to enjoy the last laugh.

In 2003, *Bad* came in at 202 on *Rolling Stone*'s 500 Greatest Albums of All Time and, in 2009, reached No. 43 of the 100 Greatest Albums Of All Time of the MTV Generation. Its reputation continues to grow. Listening to the lyrics, Michael had clearly grown up by then. But would he ever find the peace of mind he so eagerly sought?

CHAPTER SEVEN

FINDING NEVERLAND

His now truly immense wealth meant that Michael was able to buy a spectacular property: 5225 Figueroa Mountain Road, the ranch that would become Neverland. Based in Santa Ynez, California, the 3,000-acre estate was to be both a refuge from the world's prying eyes and an entertainment park for children. For all who doubted Michael Jackson was the child within a man he said he was, here was the ultimate truth. It is said that extremely famous people remain fixed, in some way, at the age at which they achieve fame and in Michael's case, he was 11 years of age when that breakthrough came.

If you were to give an 11-year-old boy an almost unlimited amount of money, this is what he would have spent it on: an estate featuring an amusement park and a zoo. There was a Ferris wheel; fairground rides including a carousel, a zipper, a spider, a sea dragon, a wave swinger, a superslide and dodgems. Michael's growing collection of animals was housed in the zoo, although Bubbles, of course, continued to share the main residence. A huge floral clock outside the front door had Neverland spelt out above it and two railroad tracks crisscrossed the grounds, with a steam engine to take visitors around. There was a cinema, and within the house itself, on the top floor was a huge room featuring a child's paradise: toys of every conceivable description. In total, there were about 22 buildings, including the main house, guesthouses, ranch-hand apartments and stables.

Michael bought the house in 1988 from the golf course entrepreneur William Bone. The exact purchase price remains unknown, although it has been reported as being anything from $16.5 million to $30 million. Whatever the original price, it was an excellent investment, being worth several hundred million by the time of his death.

It was a beautiful part of the world. About 100 miles north of Los Angeles, the surrounding area was filled with cattle ranches among the rolling hills. Celebrity neighbours included Bo Derek, Kelly LeBrock and Cheryl Ladd. The nearest town, 5 miles away, was Los Olivos. To get to it, you left the estate and drove down Figueroa Mountain Road.

Michael became very popular in the area: not only did he employ numerous locals on the estate, but he was very generous in other ways too. Just a few of the charitable acts he carried out include building a new gym for Los Olivos Elementary School and purchasing strollers for a local day-care centre. He also had a personal fire and rescue squad, which he frequently allowed the local people to use.

'He's a nice guy, probably the nicest guy you'll ever meet,' said a local man, Flynt Cody, interviewed several years before Michael's death. 'He's very neighbourly.'

Michael was to make Neverland a haven for children. He would invite them round to make full use of the fairground and even gave guided tours sometimes. As the adult world increasingly forced itself upon him, Michael retreated further and further back to the haven where no one could touch him: security was extremely tight, with guards patrolling the grounds and 'No Trespassing' signs everywhere. The situation was also helped by the fact that from the road, Neverland was completely hidden from view. After dark, a rescue squad vehicle patrolled the border of the ranch.

No one could touch him psychologically, either. The company of children was considerably simpler than that of adults: unlike his peers, they were not competitive, didn't try to do him down and revelled in his company. Michael's love of children was to get him into terrible trouble, but as with his love of animals, it was actually very easy to explain.

Michael endeared himself to the local community still further by inviting them round on special occasions. He also used his home for fundraising events. At one point he held a $5,000-a-couple bash to raise funds for his Make A Wish foundation, something that made quite an impression on those who attended the event. Farah Pajuheshfar, 45, a hairdresser based in Las Vegas, was one, along with her 12-year-old daughter, Julie.

'When we went into Neverland, I thought I had died and gone to paradise,' Farah recalled. 'The whole day we were there, from 9am until 3am, we had drinks, popcorn, candy, ice cream. There was even an open bar. The zoo was filled with elephants, giraffes, llamas, chimps, crocodiles, snakes, parrots and a black bear. It was an adventure I will never forget. If I die now, it would be OK!'

'It was a lot of fun,' Julie added. 'We went on the Ferris wheel and the roller coaster and the arcade. All the people working at Neverland were smiling all the time. I came home smiling at everybody in school.'

Michael would host a number of major events there, too: Neverland was where Elizabeth Taylor's 1991 wedding to construction worker Larry Fortensky, 20 years her junior, took place. Michael was the best man.

Increasingly, Michael needed a place to retreat from the world. Now all that was stable and familiar was receding; he no longer saw a great deal of his family and was moving away from the religion he had been brought up in: Jehovah's Witnesses. The trouble began some years earlier with the filming of *Thriller* when elders in the church expressed horror at the scenes of Michael turning into a werewolf and tried to persuade him to have the video withdrawn. He refused to do so, but compromised by putting the now-famous disclaimer at the front: 'Due to my strong personal convictions, I wish to state that the film in no way endorses a belief in the occult – Michael Jackson.'

In the immediate aftermath of the affair, Michael had been so shaken that he decided never to make another film like it. 'I would never do it again,' he said in an interview in 1984. 'I just intended to do a good, fun short film, not to purposely bring to the screen something to scare people or to do anything bad. I want to do what's right. I would never do anything like that again... because a lot of people were offended by it. That makes me feel bad. I don't want them to feel that way. I realise now that it wasn't a good idea. I'll never do a video like that again. In fact, I have blocked further distribution of the film over which I have control, including its release in some other countries. There's all kinds of promotional stuff being proposed on "Thriller" but I tell them, "No, no, no! I don't want to do anything on "Thriller." No more "Thriller."'

But by 1987, his views had changed quite dramatically and he let it be known that he no longer wished to be regarded as a Jehovah's Witness. He 'disassociated' himself from the congregation where he'd previously worshipped, causing a furore at the time and stirring up potential problems within his own family. Katherine was still a devout Jehovah's Witness and as such, technically no longer supposed to speak to her son, although clearly she ignored that and continued to provide unstinting support. Michael never went public on his reasons for doing so, but over the years, he would flirt with other faiths in an attempt to find peace. None really helped.

By the late eighties, there was also an increasing awareness that Michael did not appear ever to have had a close relationship with a woman of his own age. He had known another child star, Brooke Shields, since both of them had been in their teens and they were sometimes photographed together, leading to speculation that they were a couple. Indeed, Michael fuelled this gossip when he told Oprah Winfrey that they dated from time to time: in truth, however, that interview took place in 1993 when Michael and Brooke hadn't seen one another for a couple of years. However, they remained friends and Brooke went on to speak at Michael's memorial service.

She also revealed in an interview after his death that Michael proposed to her on a number of occasions, not, it would appear, in order to lead a conventional married life, but to assure himself he wouldn't lose her. Brooke turned him down, but the friendship deepened. 'I would say, "You have me for the rest of your life, you don't need to marry me. I'm going to go on and do my own life and have my own marriage and my own kids, and you'll always have me,"' she told *Rolling Stone* magazine. 'I think it made him relax. He didn't want to lose things that meant something to him.'

Indeed, unlike the women who were desperate to get close to their idol, Brooke never found Michael physically attractive, relating that in many ways, they never rose above the level of childhood friends. 'You saw women who were more sexual, who wanted to throw themselves at him and feel like they were going to teach him,' she recalls, 'We just found each other, and we didn't have to deal with our sexuality. As I grew up and started having boyfriends, I would share with him and he was like a little kid who talked about the bases – what first base was, what second base was, and it sounded very odd to the outside, I can imagine, but to the inside, to someone who's never really left his bubble, you can understand how he would be curious.'

At the time of the *Bad* tour, Michael was 29 and his management allowed it to become known that he was still a virgin. This must have been with Michael's consent, given both his tour manager, Chris Telvitt, and

Quincy Jones spoke out. Rumours were actually doing the rounds that Michael was gay: that, said Telvitt, was also untrue. 'He's not interested in finding a girlfriend – or a boyfriend,' he said. 'There's a big question mark over Michael's sexuality. He's got to be the oldest virgin in rock and roll. Michael is frightened of gold diggers; he can't just go into a bar and pick up a girl. He finds it impossible to relate either to women or men of his own age. He thinks he's boring, despite the fact that he is immensely talented and fantastically successful. He can only get on with older people – that's why he tags along with Liz Taylor and Sophia Loren. They present no threat to him and no challenge; they don't want to take him to bed. They just accept him for what he is.'

Quincy also took a view. 'The truth is that Michael is not interested in girls and sex,' he said. 'He is definitely still a virgin and doesn't believe he has missed anything. I suppose being Michael Jackson is compensation enough.'

And that, of course, is how he remained. Although Michael went on to marry twice, and Lisa Marie Presley called him a 'passionate lover', what Michael always appeared to be searching for in women was someone who would look after him. The little boy lost pose was not an act: Steven Spielberg once described him as, 'like a fawn in a burning forest.' It was a very apt summary and would remain so until the end of his life.

However, it must be said that by this stage, he was also an extremely financially astute fawn. Michael was doing one deal after another, from the mega-bucks Pepsi deal, the largest-ever advertising promo using a star at that stage, to the purchase of the Beatles' back catalogue and, of course, Neverland. Meanwhile, sales of *Thriller* continued to soar, and *Bad* was bringing in the cash, too. Michael had become an incredibly rich man. Why did he carry on pushing himself so hard? After all, he could have retired and never worked again.

'Rich people don't consider themselves ever having enough because they have to compete,' said Stuart Backerman, Michael's publicist between 2002 and 2004. 'They have to feel richer. Rich people – and when I'm talkin' rich, I'm talkin' really rich, not somebody who lives in Dunbar or something – they always have to keep up with the Joneses, they always have to have bigger and better. Celebrities are the same way. You can't have enough money.

'Michael liked to brag before Oprah that he was a billionaire. He wasn't satisfied with the Beatles' catalogue and making oodles of money with Pepsi commercials or anything else. He did the Pepsi commercial because a) it was a great publicity vehicle as a follow-up to *Thriller*, and just as importantly, for the moolah. Nobody's going to throw away $5 million in 1985 or '86, or whenever that was; he wasn't a fool.

Certainly at that point he may have had many of the problems and torment that he had from his childhood situation, but he was still pretty right on in those days, he was in the heyday. So he took the opportunity as it came to him.

'He wasn't shy about negotiating a $250 million deal – you know what I'm saying? People will go for what they can get, notwithstanding that they're so wealthy already. To me, the money part of Michael was part of his undoing as well. Because when you have so much money, you become profligate and that's what happened to him. And frankly, to a lot of wealthy people, they just get caught up in the material side and they don't nourish their spiritual side enough. Michael was always searching. He tried Judaism, he grew up as a Jehovah's Witness; he played with Islam although he never really believed in it... His brother very much did, Jermaine. He played with various other spiritual activities, but he never saw the goodness and the wisdom that comes from within yourself, not from outside, you know?'

At that stage, however, no one would have believed the problems that lay ahead and in 1987, the record-breaking Bad World Tour kicked off. It was Michael's first solo tour and as a result, the pressure on him was enormous; there might have been drawbacks to touring with his brothers, but at least someone else was there to share the strain. Now, Michael had to carry the whole show and while he certainly didn't have any problems in doing so, nonetheless this was an extraordinary achievement. By the time it came to an end, in January 1989, the Bad World Tour had garnered two new entries in the *Guinness Book Of Records*: for the largest-grossing tour in history, at $125 million, and also the tour with the largest attended audience. At that time, there were just 54 concerts held in the US, but even so it became the sixth largest grossing tour in 1988-9, coming in at $20.3 million and narrowly losing out on the inaugural International Rock Awards' Tour of the Year to Amnesty International. In short, it was a spectacular success.

Of course nothing that Michael did could go uncommented on, and so a great deal of attention was paid to the fact that he grabbed his crotch a lot in those days, when he danced. For a time it became a matter of some debate: it didn't quite fit in with Michael's über-innocent image and concern was expressed by some parents that he might be leading their tots astray. Even the man himself couldn't really explain it. 'I think it happens subliminally,' he told Oprah Winfrey. 'When you're dancing, you know, you are just interpreting the music and the sounds and the accompaniment. If there's a driving base, if there's a cello, if there's a string, you become the emotion of what the sound is.

'So if I'm doing a movement and I go "Bam!" and I

grab myself, it's... it's the music that compels me to do it. It's not that I'm saying that I'm dying to grab down there and it's not in a great place. You don't think about it, it just happens. Sometimes I'll look back at the footage and I go... and I go, "Did I do that?" so I'm a slave to the rhythm.'

By now he was donating huge amounts of cash and throughout the tour, he made sure that tickets were set aside for underprivileged children: from hospitals, orphanages and so forth. He also distributed some of the profits from the tour to charity. It opened in Japan, 1987, where it caused a sensation, earning Michael the nickname, 'Typhoon Michael'. When Michael and Bubbles, travelling in different jets, arrived at Narita International Airport in Tokyo, over 600 journalists alone were waiting for them, and that's before counting the fans. To give some idea of the scale of the venture, another jumbo accompanied them with 22 truckloads of stage equipment and tour-related paraphernalia: the number of people in the tour entourage was 132.

The Japanese leg of the tour was marked by one happening after another. Michael was deeply touched to hear about a 5-year-old boy, Yoshioka Hagiwara, who had recently been kidnapped and murdered. He dedicated the Japanese leg to him, along with every performance of 'I Just Can't Stop Loving You', donating £12,000 to the child's parents. He was given the key to Osaka by the then mayor Yasushi Oshima. In a first for any animal, Bubbles was allowed to accompany his owner inside the town hall. One of Emperor Hirohito's granddaughters also attended a concert. Ultimately, total attendance for the 14 Japanese concerts was 450,000, which knocked the previous record of 200,000 into a hat.

Although Michael received a rapturous reception wherever he went, concerns continued to be raised about the state of his health. His skin was noticeably paler than it had been previously, a condition he later told Oprah Winfrey was caused by vitiligo, a common skin disorder in which patches of skin lose their colour when the pigmentation breaks down. His nose was considerably more slender and his face appeared more feminine still. He was also slimmer than ever before. The press speculated openly that he was bleaching his skin and wanted to be white, something Michael only finally addressed some years later when talking to Oprah.

'OK, but number one, this is the situation,' he declared. 'I have a skin disorder that destroys the pigmentation of my skin. It's something that I cannot help, OK? But when people make up stories that I don't want to be what I am, it hurts me... It's a problem for me that I can't control... But what about all the millions of people who sit out in the sun to become darker, to become other than what they are? No one says nothing about that!'

Oprah pressed him further. 'It's in my family, my father said it's on his side,' he insisted. 'I can't control it, I don't understand. I mean it makes me very sad. I don't want to go into my medical history because that is private, but that's the situation here.'

'So, OK, I just want to get this straight: you are not taking anything to change the colour of your skin?' asked Oprah.

'Oh God, no! We tried to control it and using make-up evens it out because it makes blotches on my skin,' explained Michael. 'I have to even out my skin.'

It must be said that he was not being entirely straightforward about the change in the way he looked. He admitted to some plastic surgery, two nose jobs and the cleft in the chin, but clearly he must have had much, much more done. Years later, a documentary was made about his changing appearance and the producers enlisted the help of New York-based plastic surgeon Dr. Pamela Lipkin to analyse his face over the years. She was initially shown a photograph of Michael as a child. 'At that point, Michael Jackson's [a] very normal, very cute, Afro-American child, with actually very good features,' she remarked. 'You know, good lips, high cheekbones, good bone structure... Even skin tone, I might add.'

She then looked at a picture of him with Diana Ross at a charity gig when he was just 24. 'Obviously he's had some nasal surgery,' she commented. 'The width of the nostrils is dramatically reduced... The bridge is much thinner... And you know something? That's a great result. Having started with that nose, that nose is still believable.'

But by the time of *Bad*, the changes were becoming quite significant. 'His eyebrows are very, very high, so he's probably had some sort of forehead lift or brow lift,' she continued. 'His eyes, I'm not sure. He probably did have some fat removed around his eyes. They're particularly naked-looking. That's not a natural cleft; you can tell.' Lipkin knew of a technique for creating a cleft chin, she said, but that it was not popular because, 'it never looks real.'

Meanwhile, the *Bad* tour moved on. After a stint in Australia, where Michael was nicknamed Crocodile Jackson, and sang 'Just Good Friends' with Stevie Wonder, who made a surprise guest appearance on stage, the juggernaut flew to the US. There was some substantial redesign, including the costumes. According to one member of the crew, Michael, 'thought he was wearing too much leather back then [during the first leg] and looked a bit ridiculous. So he grew his hair, threw away his jacket and strapped on a massive belt. The result makes him look raw and street-wise.'

The show dazzled in the States, just as it had in Japan. In a way, the sense of pride was even greater: the people of America, after all, were flocking to see one of their own and the event garnered the most spectacular reviews. 'In the Jackson version of pop, the dancing is as important as the singing and the look is probably most important of all,' wrote Stephen Holden in the *New York Times*. 'Jackson was the first pop star of the television age. We are in the twilight of the pop video at the moment; this was an age that Michael Jackson ushered in and dominated, despite the reluctance of MTV to show clips of performers of colour.

'I saw him perform at Madison Square Garden in 1988 during the high noon of his dominance. The show was kitsch, dazzling, rehearsed within an inch of its life and built for an MTV attention span. (Returning to the hotel, I shared a lift with his chimp, Bubbles. Neither of us batted an eyelid. This was obviously how the game was to be played from then on.)'

Michael was certainly doing his bit for the less privileged, too. He was giving large amounts to charity. In March 1988, he performed at a private concert in Madison Square Garden, from which all the proceeds went to the United Negro College Fund. Four years earlier, when he was on the Victory Tour, the UNCF had created the Michael Jackson Scholars program and by that time 78 students had received a Michael Jackson scholarship. The plaudits continued to pour in: Michael was awarded an Honorary Doctorate of Humane Letters Degree from Fisk University and the Frederik D.

Patterson Award in the wake of his contribution to UNCF. He was clearly trying to pass on the benefits of his own good fortune.

In the course of the concert Tatiana Thumbtzen (who worked with Michael on the video for 'The Way You Make Me Feel') kissed him. Naturally, this sparked rumours of a romance. The world, it seemed, now actively wanted the superstar to settle down. But the full extent of the damage done to him during his childhood had still not become clear: despite the marriages, Michael would never really be able to enjoy that aspect of life. In any case, doing good deeds was obviously bringing him some fulfilment: by the time he got the Atlanta, Georgia, he gave away 100 tickets to the Children's Wish Foundation for terminally ill children.

That same month, Michael appeared at the Grammy Awards at Radio City Hall in Los Angeles. It was his first appearance on TV for five years, the first since the Motown sensation in 1983. Michael didn't actually win any Grammys, but he put in a performance of such polish and aplomb that he got a standing ovation for 'Man In The Mirror' and 'The Way You Make Me Feel'. Many believed this was actually the best performance ever seen at the Grammy awards. But again, it was overshadowed by past greatness: while the Motown appearance has gone down in history, this one has always been slightly overlooked, perhaps because there are only so many superlatives you can throw at one man. As for the lack of Grammys, many took the view that this was due to some sort of backlash, with Michael having scooped so many, last time around. Anyway, there were plenty of other awards for him to revel in, including four Billboard awards, three NAACP awards, two Soul Train awards and the MTV Video Vanguard Award for Outstanding Contribution to Music Video Production. It wasn't as if his achievement had gone entirely unnoticed.

The tour moved on to Europe. In Italy, Michael showed faint signs of cabin fever and snuck out of his hotel, the Lord Byron Hotel, wearing a wig, false moustache and raincoat. While his staff panicked and searched the city for him, Michael returned by taxi. It was very rare for him to take such a risk – wherever he went, he was mobbed and this could have turned nasty – but clearly, he felt the need to experience life outside the confines of how he now lived, just for an hour or so. His charitable donations continued, too: he donated £100,000 to the Bambino Gesu Hospital, one of the leading children's hospitals in Italy. The charabanc moved on.

Wherever Michael went, there was a heavy celebrity attendance in tow and really big names, too. When he played Basel, Switzerland, two members of the audience were Elizabeth Taylor and Bob Dylan. But a Michael

Jackson concert was an event. Michael was absolutely at the peak of his powers in every way: the energy he displayed on stage was quite astonishing; the special effects and pyrotechnics jaw-dropping and the element of surprise kept the audience constantly wondering what would happen next.

While all this was going on, the singles kept mounting up. In April 1988, the fifth single from the album, *Dirty Diana*, came out (some mischievous voices said this referred to Princess Diana) and achieved pop music history by going straight to No. 1. Michael became the first artist to have achieved five No. 1 singles from one album. The next one, 'Another Part Of Me', came out in the July and only reached No. 11, but by that time, frankly, who cared? It seemed there was no touching him, no stopping him now.

Finally, he reached Wembley Stadium in London, where there were 1.5 million applications for tickets, which would have sold out the 72,000-venue 20 times over. Celebrities flocked to see him, including Shirley Bassey, Jack Nicholson and Frank Bruno. Michael then met Prince Charles and Princess Diana. 'I can give you some dance lessons,' he informed Prince Charles, before telling an interviewer, 'For different people, growing up can occur at a different age and now I'm showing the world that I'm the man I always wanted to be.'

After the concert, Michael gave Princess Diana *Bad*

tour jackets for her two young sons, William and Harry. The two established a friendship that was to endure until her death, nearly a decade later, in 1997. 'We would talk about everything that was happening in her life,' Michael later recalled. 'She needed to talk to someone who knew exactly what she was going through. She felt hunted in the way I've felt hunted. Trapped, if you like. You can't talk about that to your neighbour because how would they ever understand?' Her death, 'was the saddest I've ever felt. It broke my heart; I just cried and cried.'

The charitable donations continued. Michael presented Prince Charles and Princess Diana with a cheque for £300,000, the proceeds from the Wembley concerts, to go to the charitable organisation, The Prince's Trust, which helped disadvantaged young people find a way in life. The adoration of the public just grew: when Michael moved on to Leeds and found himself onstage on 29 August, the date of his 30th birthday, the audience serenaded him with 'Happy Birthday'.

There were an astonishing two more singles from the album, 'Leave Me Alone' (the title indicates that Michael might occasionally have found all the attention hard to deal with) and 'Liberian Girl', which he dedicated to Elizabeth Taylor. By this stage, the album itself had sold 17 million copies, although ultimately it would notch up 32 million in sales. Michael ended the year by taking part in various events for the showbiz elite: he appeared on the Sammy Davis Jr 60th Anniversary TV special, performing a song he had written specially for the occasion, 'You Were There'.

At the Soul Train Awards, Michael was presented with a gong by his old friend Elizabeth Taylor: the Sammy Davis Jr Award and Heritage Award. There, she gave him a title that exists to this day. Michael, she said, was the King of Pop. He certainly was that. Fans took up the nickname and ran with it, chanting the title outside his hotels and hoisting banners bearing the legend during his concerts. No one else could touch him. Now Michael was truly in a class of his own, one that has remained unequalled.

CHAPTER EIGHT
THE MOONWALKER

The *Bad* world tour had been a spectacular success, but Michael now wanted to spend some time on his newly acquired ranch, back in America. But, as ever during that stage of his life, he had plenty of projects on the boil. One of these was his autobiography called, naturally, *Moon Walk*. It went on to sell 200,000 copies and got to the top of the *New York Times* Best Sellers list in 1988. The person who actually penned the book was Stephen David, an experienced rock and roll biographer, who spent about 20 hours talking with Michael about his life. Michael's editor, at his own insistence, was another global icon: Jackie Kennedy Onassis.

In an interview with the *Boston Globe* after Michael's death, Stephen David was asked if he enjoyed Michael's music. 'Sure,' he replied. 'As a music fan and former editor of *Rolling Stone*, I knew those records. *Off the Wall* is one of the greatest records ever. I've been driving around this morning and the radio stations are blasting his stuff. Sounds great.'

Like so much that Michael was involved with, however, the book's production was not without controversy. Despite the fact that he had formed close, warm relationships with other women of a certain age who were, like him, globally famous, Michael's relationship with Jackie O would ultimately turn sour. She felt more than a little pushed around by Michael and he, meanwhile, was insistent they do everything exactly his way. 'Michael made her write the foreword,' said Stephen. 'He basically extorted it from her; she didn't want to do it. She was reticent to lend her name to anything, but he made her write it. She thought it was an intrusion and unprofessional. Then he wouldn't let a paperback come out, so that sort of killed the relationship.'

Despite this, the book went on to become a roaring success. Much of the work was done before Michael moved to Neverland, at the family compound in Encino. Clearly, this provided something of a template for the home Michael was going to create for himself. 'He was a 29-year-old kid who had more money than God,' recalled Stephen. 'It was a fabulously extravagant compound, complete with a zoo, a candy store, swimming pools, movie theater, playground, basketball courts. It was fantasy, like a miniature Disney. It was really cool... The living room... was like a reception hall of some Saudi Arabian prince. There were chandeliers, fabulously expensive carpets... Sometimes, a girl would come in and listen. That was Janet. Only Michael and Janet were living there at the time.'

By then, Michael had formed his habit of having friendships with small boys, something that would have terrible consequences, but Stephen was adamant nothing untoward went on. At that time, Michael was friendly with a boy called Rubba and Stephen witnessed the two together. 'I never saw anything,' he said. 'And no vibe at all. Rubba was like a little leaguer – I wonder where he is today? "Rubba, go get us two Ring Dings and a soda."'

Stephen also met another famous individual, one with whom Michael spent a great deal of his time. 'Early on, Michael invited my family over for lunch,' he related. 'My daughter Lily was seven years old and I asked Michael if there was any way she could meet Bubbles. Five minutes later, Bubbles shows up, holding the hand of his trainer. I guess the monkey didn't see too many girls because he grabbed Lily's hand and started dragging her out of the room. Michael then grabbed the other hand and Lily became the rope in a tug of war between Michael and Bubbles. Michael said, "Bubbles, where are you going with my girlfriend?" Finally, the trainer took out some sort of buzzer, a tiny little cattleprod, and zapped Bubbles.'

Stephen also saw the oxygen chamber that it had been claimed Michael had slept in. 'He didn't get into it, but I saw the hyperbaric chamber,' he explained. 'It was near the bedroom. Michael had incredible stuff: the complete Sun Records 45s, the complete Beatles... That was when he owned Paul McCartney's ass and wanted to make money by licensing Beatles' songs... Michael was a really good guy, but it was almost like he'd been hermetically sealed. I would say this: everything you've heard about Michael Jackson is true, except the molestation stuff.'

In the book, Michael admits to some minor plastic surgery, but also goes much further, disclosing for the first time the extent of the problems and difficulties he suffered as a child. This came as a shock. Michael had, in some ways, such a sunny nature and childlike sense of puzzlement with the world that it simply hadn't occurred to most people that he might have suffered problems as a child. This did, however, begin to explain why he retained a childlike quality and why he was so obsessed with helping children.

Back then, before the first allegations of abuse were made against him, his reputation was entirely philanthropic. For years now, he had been making substantial donations to children's charities and it was well known that he enjoyed children's games and the preoccupations of children, such as funfair rides and zoos. Even Bubbles showed that Michael had not really grown up: to spend his time with a chimpanzee rather than people of his own age was a sure sign that something was setting him apart.

Neverland was to come to represent that, too. In the wake of Michael's death, journalists were allowed access to the building. One of them was Christopher Hawthorne, architecture critic of the *Los Angeles Times*: 'It was while I was bumpily making my way across a rope bridge in a quiet corner of Michael Jackson's Neverland Ranch on Thursday morning – next to an elaborate treehouse crowned with a ship's wheel, and overlooking a bronze sculpture of smiling children – that I finally figured out what the late entertainer's compound represents from an architectural point of view... At the height of his popularity, Jackson bent the music industry toward an androgynous, perpetually childlike model of superstardom. He managed a similar trick in transforming the architecture of this classic Santa Barbara County ranch property.'

That same year, Michael released the film *Moonwalker*. Originally planned to coincide with the release of *Bad*, *Moonwalker* actually came out just as the world tour drew to a close. It is, in essence, a series of short films about Michael Jackson, mainly set to the music from *Bad*. Opening with 'Man In The Mirror', the central segment is based on 'Smooth Criminal', in which Michael plays a good-guy gangster, who variously transforms himself into a car and a spaceship, saving a group of children (including Sean Lennon) from the evil Mr. Big, played by Joe Pesci as a tongue-in-cheek parody of the American music industry executive Frank DiLeo.

The work received a rather mixed reception. '*Moonwalker* – also the title of a Michael Jackson autobiography – seems unsure of what it was supposed to be,' said *Variety* magazine. 'At the center of the pic is the "Smooth Criminal" segment, a musical/dramatic piece full of dancing, schmaltzy kids, sci-fi effects and blazing machine guns [directed by Colin Chilvers, based on a story by Jackson]. Around it are really just numerous Jackson music videos with little or no linkage. Although quite enjoyable, the whole affair does not make for a structured or professional movie.'

'Released in 1988, *Moonwalker* was a feature-length film starring Michael Jackson that was cut up into several different short films, most of which were long-form music videos used to promote his *Bad* album,' was the verdict of *Fandango*. 'During one memorable scene, Jackson transforms into a robot in order to save some children (including Sean Lennon) from the evil Mr. Big (played by Joe Pesci). Perhaps it's not how Michael Bay would've directed the scene, but it's interesting nonetheless to watch.'

The 1980s really was Michael's decade. Although he would go on to score further major successes, he was then at the height of his powers and it's the time for which he will always be remembered. Fittingly, as the decade drew to a close, he became the first Westerner to appear in a TV advertisement in the Soviet Union – the Cold War was ending and the first person to cross those boundaries, from West to East, was probably the most famous Western performer ever.

At the end of the eighties, more honours were showered upon Michael. Elizabeth Taylor anointed him 'King of Pop' when she gave him the Artist of the Decade award in 1989 and President Bush presented him with the White House's special Artist of the Decade award. It seemed everything he touched turned to gold; his star could not have glowed more brightly, had it tried.

The new decade started pretty well, too. First, in 1991, Michael played host to his great friend Elizabeth Taylor's $2 million wedding to former construction worker Larry Fortensky at Neverland. Michael gave Elizabeth away, and the occasion was as spectacular as might be expected. Up to 80 security guards kept intruders out as Michael walked Elizabeth up a wooden walkway to the gazebo in which the ceremony was held. The 59-year-old bride was clad in a $30,000 yellow gown, while the groom, 39, sported a tuxedo. Also in attendance was English actor Roddy McDowall, one of Elizabeth's closest friends: both he and Elizabeth wept during the ceremony. Matters were only marred slightly when a journalist carrying a camera parachuted into the proceedings, landing just 100 feet away from the gazebo; he was led away in disgrace, and in chains.

At the end of the ceremony, a flock of white doves was released before the happy couple sailed round a swan-filled lake in a boat fashioned to look like a swan. A trio of violinists serenaded them as they retired to a candlelit wing of the main house; outside three bands entertained guests as they dined on salmon and champagne.

The acclaimed American fashion photographer Herb Ritts took pictures of the occasion while gossip columnist Liz Smith filed her own report: 'She did it!' Liz wrote in her *Newsday* column. 'In spite of 15 maddening helicopters overhead that totally drowned out the words of her marriage ceremony, and the parachutist who landed within 20 feet of the minister in the middle of the wedding, Elizabeth the Queen took as her consort last evening commoner and construction worker Larry Fortensky.' Alas, the marriage would last just 40 months and the couple divorced in 1996, following a trial separation.

Rather more importantly, Michael's career was going from strength to strength. In September 1991, he broke another record, this time for achieving the best-paid recording contract ever made to that date, for $65 million. This allowed him enormous creative leeway, in as many media as he cared to entertain. Back then, no other artist in the world was more successful and so it made sense for Sony, just as much as it did for Michael himself.

'The deal we made – and I don't think it's appropriate to discuss the details – we think is economic for us,' stated Michael P. Schulhof, then vice chairman of Sony U.S.A, in *Rolling Stone* magazine in 1992 (Michael made the cover, just as he had intended). 'If Michael continues to perform the way he has in the past, both he and we will do very well. He's 33 years old. I don't think anybody, including Michael himself, can predict how he is going to exercise that creativity. It may be in music, it may be in film; it may be in totally new areas of entertainment. The fact that the contract with him is unique reflects the fact that he is a unique talent.'

The first album to appear as a result of the new agreement was *Dangerous*, in 1991. Made for a reputed $10 million (the industry norm was about $2 million at that time), the cover featured a picture of Michael's eyes, with the rest of his face obscured by a surreal illustration by the artist Mark Ryden. On Quincy Jones' recommendation, it was produced by Bill Bottrell and Teddy Riley, who invented a new style of music called

New Jack Swing, or Swingbeat and fused the production techniques of hip hop with the sound of R&B. Although the album didn't receive quite the critical acclaim of *Bad* or *Thriller*, it was massively successful, more so than *Bad* – in fact, to date it has sold around 32 million copies worldwide. Like *Bad*, it went in at No. 1 on the Billboard Charts, following release on 26 November 1991, which is where it spent the next four weeks.

Recording took place at Ocean Way/Record One studio and Larrabee Studios North. The album actually took much longer to make than its predecessors and one of the reasons for the very high costs involved was that the two studios were booked full-time, whether or not they were being used. It was an early example of an extravagance that was to veer out of control, although Michael was making so much money for himself and everyone else back then that no one got a proper grip. It is estimated that he earned an unbelievable sum of $175 million from sales of the album alone, excluding other add-ons in his contract with Sony, or the singles or videos.

Even so, a certain amount of profligacy was noted. 'Usually, there wasn't a whole lot going on in any of the studios unless Michael was there,' a source who worked on the album revealed to *Rolling Stone* magazine shortly after it came out.

'When they were at Larrabee, they still had Record

One booked. It's a little eccentric. Nobody makes records like that. It would be fun to be able to spend that kind of money, I'll tell you. It's just 'cos he has so much other stuff going on. Trying to help kids. Like, if all of a sudden up in Sacramento someone shoots a bunch of kids, he has to go up there and spend time with them. There was a lot of that stuff going on every day. Every day he'd want to go do something else. There were a lot of distractions. Liz is getting married, and he goes and deals with that, but still the studios were booked.'

Initially, a greatest hits album (*Decade*) had been planned, with some new material added in. But in typical Michael fashion, there was so much new material, of such high quality (like *Bad*, the album was to generate nine singles), that in the end the decision was made to release it as an entirely new work.

'I wanted to do an album that was like Tchaikovsky's *Nutcracker Suite*,' said Michael in an interview with *Ebony* magazine, displaying knowledge of different musical *oeuvres* that might have surprised some. 'So that in a thousand years from now, people would still be listening to it; something that would live forever. I would like to see children and teenagers and parents and all races all over the world, hundreds and hundreds of years from now, still pulling out songs from that album and dissecting it. I want it to live.'

By now, Michael was working a new crew, in a period

of intense creativity. In some ways, this would be the last time that he could work in a relatively carefree environment. Although he was to issue further albums, this was the last one before his name was dragged into the mire. Creatively, he was at the top of his game and producer Teddy Riley enjoyed every minute of the making of *Dangerous*.

'Michael likes to listen even louder than me,' Riley told *Rolling Stone*. 'His volume is past twelve. I'm maybe nine or ten. His volume is twelve-plus. Oh, man, he loves loud music. And he jams! Only way you know your music is right is if he's dancing all over the studio. He starts going, "Yeah, whoa!" When the deadline came, he wanted to do more and more songs. And his manager came in there and said, "Teddy, you and Michael, you're not up to your sneaky stuff. Do not write another song." And then when Michael saw the commercial for *Dangerous*, the David Lynch thing, we started working hard to get it finished.' Comments such as this make it clear how the stash of unpublished material came to light around the time of Michael's death: he had been building it up for years.

In fact, Michael told *Ebony* just how many of the numbers came about. 'I wrote "Will You Be There" at my house, Neverland in California... I didn't think about it hard,' he said. 'That's why it's hard to take credit for the songs that I write, because I just always feel that it's done from above. I feel fortunate for being that instrument through which music flows. I'm just the source through which it comes. I can't take credit for it because it's God's work. He's just using me as the messenger.'

The first single to be released from the album was Michael's most successful since 'Billie Jean': 'Black or White' (ironically, Michael was now so pale he could quite easily pass for the latter). It's a song about racial harmony and, according to producer Bill Bottrell, it originated from something that Michael had been working on for *Bad*, which he decided to develop further. 'That piece of music, the beginning part that Slash plays on, was first recorded at Michael's house,' he recalled. 'Michael asked me to dig it out of the vault in August of 1989. He had in mind to use it as the intro to "Black Or White". It took a long time before we got Slash on it.' And when they did, Michael was not actually present at the recording: 'He [Slash] was disappointed. He was frustrated that Michael wasn't there.'

The accompanying video was to be Michael's most controversial work since *Thriller*. Like *Thriller*, groundbreaking special effects were employed, in this case the technique of morphing, in which one image 'morphs' into another, but a four-minute segment at the end caused outcry. It started conventionally enough, with Macaulay Culkin, one of the most famous American child stars, using loudspeakers to blast his father (George Wendt, aka Norm Peterson from *Cheers*) across the world to Africa, where he encounters Michael singing about various cultures and morphing into black panthers and the like.

In hindsight, it might be claimed that Michael was beginning to suffer a severe internal conflict that, in truth, would never be fully resolved. While craving the success that he was reaping so massively, at the same time he was starting to find the constant attention almost intolerable. No one could have survived untouched in a goldfish bowl like that, let alone a person whose security and self-belief had been so fundamentally undermined at such a young age, and signs that Michael may have been feeling the strain were now coming through loud and clear.

In the final segment, Michael prowls out of the studio in the guise of a black panther and then morphs into himself. He then did more crotch grabbing and trouser zipping than ever before and compounded matters further by smashing the windows of a car and destroying an inn. According to Michael himself, this was an example of the panther's animalistic behaviour.

However, others found this totally unacceptable and there was a general outcry. After all, Michael had a legion of very young fans and for them to see their hero indulging in such anti-social behaviour was not on. He had a clean-living image, too and now that was also

Above: The Neverland Valley Ranch, Michael's private residence in California.

Below: The amusement park at Neverland. Amongst other things, it included fairground rides and a zoo.

In 1994, Michael married Lisa Marie Presley, the daughter of Elvis Presley. The marriage lasted just two years.

Above Michael set up the Heal the World Foundation in 1992. He is pictured at a press conference for the Foundation (*left*) and at one of its orphanages in Romania (*right*).

Below left: Another showstopping costume for the London leg of the *Dangerous* tour in 1992.

Below right: With his sister, Janet, at the Grammy awards in 1993.

No one in the world moved quite like Michael Jackson.

Aviator sunglasses and military-style jackets formed one of Michael's signature looks. *Inset*: King of Pop meets the President – Michael with George Bush Sr.

Above: Never knowingly understated. A Michael Jackson statue arrives on a barge on the River Thames, one of many identical statues used to promote the *HIStory* tour.

Below: Performing at the Brit Awards at London's Earl's Court in 1996.

Above left: Debbie Rowe arrives in Australia – she and Michael got married on the Australian leg of the *HIStory* world tour.

Above right: The couple in France in 1997. Michael regularly wore surgical masks when out in public.

Below: Michael, Debbie and their baby son, Prince, the first of two children they would have together.

Mandela and Michael in 1999. Michael donated millions of dollars worth of proceeds from his concerts to the Nelson Mandela Children's Fund as part of his charitable work.

deemed under threat. *Entertainment Weekly* even devoted a cover to the furore that had shaken everyone to the core, under the heading, MICHAEL JACKSON'S VIDEO NIGHTMARE. Michael subsequently withdrew the footage and issued a public apology: 'It upsets me to think that "Black or White" could influence any child or adult to destructive behaviour, either sexual or violent,' he stated. 'I've always tried to be a good role model and therefore have made these changes to avoid any possibility of adversely affecting any individual's behaviour. I deeply regret any pain or hurt that the final segment of "Black or White" has caused children, their parents or any other viewers.'

But the plaudits soon flooded in again and sales continued to soar. However, by now, Michael's appearance really was beginning to spark controversy, and no matter what he said in public, in private he admitted to having changed quite a bit. Certainly, he was very open about it all to producer Teddy Riley. 'I'm quite sure if Michael could have done it all over again, he would not have done that,' stated Riley, back in 1992. 'But there's no turning back. Once you change your description, you can't turn back. You can't get your own face on your own skin back again. But he is still Michael Jackson, he is still the talented man that everybody grew up on.'

And while Michael never admitted to bleaching his

skin, there is almost no doubt that he was doing so. The vitiligo story just didn't add up.

Understandably, many of his fellow artists, especially African Americans, refused to acknowledge this. Michael Jackson was the most famous black man in the world and so it was hardly surprising they were reluctant to concede that he was so desperate to alter his racial features. But the fact was that ever since he was a child, Michael had loathed his appearance. More than anything else, this was a sign of insecurity, and not racism, that he was so clearly tampering with his own appearance.

One person who totally accepted this, and following the singer's death, discussed it openly, was Quincy Jones. 'Oh, we talked about it all the time,' he said, in the wake of Michael's death, in an interview with *Detail* magazine. 'But he'd come up with, "Man, I promise you I have this disease," and "I have a blister on my lungs," and all that bullshit. It's hard, because Michael is a Virgo, man – he's very set in his ways. You can't talk him out of it. Chemical peels and all that stuff, it's ridiculous, man. And I don't understand that. But he obviously didn't want to be black.'

Most probably it would be closer to the mark to say that Michael Jackson didn't want to be Michael Jackson. Certainly, he never referred to himself as being anything other than black, and in his 1993 interview with Oprah Winfrey, he said that he was proud of his race.

And 'Black Or White' certainly deals with those issues. Initially, the window-smashing scene had the windows adorned with racist slogans, including 'KKK Rules', 'Nigger Go Home', 'Hitler Lives' and 'No More Wetbacks'. The fact that Michael is seen smashing those slogans is a sure sign that he refused to accept them and was fighting back on behalf of his race. In the major dance sequence at the heart of the video, he encounters people of all races, before walking through a collage of fire, proclaiming, 'I ain't scared of no sheets,' a clear reference to the Ku Klux Klan.

Whatever the complexities behind it all, 'Black Or White' was a huge success. Released in the US in November 1991, it debuted on the Billboard Chart at No. 35, and by the following week, it had moved up to No. 3; it then got to No. 1, where it stayed for seven weeks. Meanwhile, Michael had duly broken another record: he was the first performer to have a No. 1 single over three decades: the 1970s, 1980s and 1990s. 'Black Or White' also broke records in the UK, where it went straight in at No. 1, the first single by an American performer to do so since Elvis's 'It's Now Or Never' in 1960. All told, it became No. 1 in 18 countries, selling over 1 million copies in the US alone.

Another eight singles were released from the album, up to the end of 1993: 'Remember The Time', 'In The Closet', 'Who Is It', 'Jam', 'Heal The World', 'Give In To

Me', 'Will You Be There' and 'Gone Too Soon'. There had been plans afoot to release 'Dangerous' – a strong track – as a single as well. A fine piece of work, the release was ultimately cancelled when the first accusations of child abuse surfaced. In the UK and elsewhere, 'Heal The World' was the best-selling single from the album and the track would become something of a signature song for Michael in later years.

By this time, he had set up his Heal the World Foundation and announced a new deal with Pepsi (asked how much Michael would receive, Pepsi's vice president for worldwide marketing, Peter Kendall, replied, 'A lot'). He also announced plans for the *Dangerous* world tour, the proceeds going to his Heal the World Foundation. According to Michael, he wanted to, 'spread the message of global love in the hope that others, too, will be moved to do their share to heal the world.'

On 27 June 1992, the *Dangerous* world tour headed off around the globe and was ongoing for the next year and a half. Despite all of the hoopla surrounding him, Michael would never enjoy such a relatively unsullied time again. In total, the tour comprised 67 concerts, playing to 3.5 million, while he also sold the broadcast rights to HBO for $20 million, a record that stands to this day.

But this time was by no means solely devoted to

touring. Michael involved himself in raising funds and awareness for AIDS, something he brought up when he performed at President Bill Clinton's Inaugural Gala. (An utterly star-struck Chelsea Clinton gaped in awe when they were on stage together, images that flashed around the world.)

Michael also paid a visit to Africa in 1992, on a non-performing tour as it were, the Back To Eden tour. He travelled around, raising awareness of poverty in Africa, but also showing his love for its people. In fact, he had first been there (to Senegal, when he was 14) and certainly related to it then: 'When we came off the plane [in Dakar], we were greeted by a long line of African dancers,' he said at the time. 'Their drums and sounds filled the air with rhythm. I was going crazy, I was screaming, "All right! They got the rhythm! This is it. This is where I come from. The origin."'

Now, as an adult, he was back. Michael's visit started in Gabon, where he got a bigger audience than Nelson Mandela. There, he accepted the Medal of Honour from President Omar Bongo, who told him he was the first entertainer to receive it; others were statesmen and politicians, including Mandela himself. He then moved on to the Ivory Coast, where more people flocked to see him than they did the Pope.

In the village of Abidjan, populated by the Agni tribe, Amon N'Djaolk, the tribal chief of the Krindjabo, placed a crown on his head and anointed him King of Sani. 'Merci beaucoup,' said a clearly overwhelmed Michael. 'Thank you very much.' He then signed official documents and sat on a golden throne while women danced before him. Anyone who thought Michael was ashamed of his race would have been hard-pushed to explain that one. He travelled on to Cairo, Egypt and Tanzania. Huge excitement followed him, wherever he went.

In the wake of his trip, he gave an intensely revealing interview to *Ebony* magazine about his feelings towards Africa, and many other aspects of his career. 'For me, its like the "dawn of civilization,"' he said. 'It's the first place where society existed. It's seen a lot of love. I guess there's that connection because it is the root of all rhythm. Everything. It's home.'

He was then asked about the difference between seeing Africa as an adult, compared to when he was 14. 'I'm more aware of things this time: the people and how they live and their government,' he said. 'But for me, I'm more aware of the rhythms and the music and the people. That's what I'm really noticing more than anything. The rhythms are incredible. You can tell, especially the way the children move. Even the little babies, when they hear the drums, they start to move: the rhythm, the way it affects their soul, and they start to move. The same thing that blacks have in America.'

The magazine also talked with him about his love of children and animals. 'Well, there's a certain sense that animals and children have that gives me a certain creative juice, a certain force that later on in adulthood is kind of lost because of the conditioning that happens in the world,' he revealed. 'A great poet said once, "When I see children, I see that God has not yet given up on man." An Indian poet from India said that, and his name is Tagore. The innocence of children represents to me the source of infinite creativity that is the potential of every human being. But by the time you are an adult, you're conditioned; you're so conditioned by the things about you – and it goes.'

Little did he know it, but Michael was creating an opportunity for those who wanted to see him go down. Before the first allegations of abuse arose, he was known for his charity, his philanthropy and his desire to do the right thing. But it was his passionate love of children that was to prove his undoing, for if there was any ground to attack Michael, this was it. To suggest quite another motive was behind his love of children would destroy him, but no one realised this at the time.

Michael's rationale behind his love of children was perfectly logical, but it was to be used against him in a dreadful way. 'Children are loving; they don't gossip, they don't complain, they're just open hearted,' he continued. 'They're ready for you. They don't judge.

They don't see things by way of color. They're very child-like. That's the problem with adults: they lose that child-like quality. And that's the level of inspiration that's so needed and is so important for creating and writing songs, and for a sculptor, a poet or a novelist.'

Indeed, he cited children as a huge inspiration for his work – not just his own relationship with them, but in the importance of attaining a childlike state. 'It's that same kind of innocence, that same level of consciousness, that you create from,' he explained. 'And kids have it. I feel it right away from animals and children, and nature, of course. And when I'm on stage, I can't perform if I don't have that kind of ping-pong with the crowd. You know the kind of cause-and-effect action, reaction, because I play off of them. They're really feeding me and I'm just acting from their energy.'

How did he see this in his work, asked *Ebony*? 'I really believe that God chooses people to do certain things, the way Michelangelo or Leonardo da Vinci, or Mozart or Muhammad Ali or Martin Luther King is chosen,' said Michael, again showing some knowledge of serious culture, though not the greatest degree of modesty in comparing himself, it must be said. 'And that is their mission to do that thing. And I think that I haven't scratched the surface yet of what my real purpose is for being here. I'm committed to my art.'

Poor Michael! Committed though he might have been,

it seemed as if the world was out to get him. Having climbed the very pinnacle of success in show business, he was about to stare right into the abyss.

CHAPTER NINE
SCANDAL

In every way, it was an absolutely spectacular performance. The Super Bowl is the highlight of the American sporting calendar: the championship game of the National Football League, the most-watched broadcast on TV. Every year, at half time, some of the world's top entertainers stage a performance, but this time it was groundbreaking as Michael was the first ever performer to be the only act in the half-time show. In January 1993, he put on the showpiece of his career.

Originally appearing on a giant screen, Michael was literally catapulted up off the screen and onto the stage as the crowd went wild: dressed in trademark military black, he held a pose for nearly a minute before kicking off his routine. Out they came, the old favourites and the new – 'Billie Jean', 'Jam', 'Heal The World' and 'Black

Or White' – as dancers joined him onstage in an amazing routine. Never had Michael appeared so energetic: he was in his element, and it showed. This became the first Super Bowl ever where viewing figures actually rose at half time: with viewers estimated at 135 million, it was no surprise that *Dangerous* shot 90 places back up the album charts.

Michael was only 34, but even so, at the Grammys that year, he was presented with the Living Legend Award. Sadly, it seems apt in many ways, for in retrospect his career would never really recover from the events that lay ahead. Regarded by many as the greatest pop star that ever lived, now he had been crowned as such. There was nowhere to go, but down.

In February 1993, Michael granted Oprah Winfrey a television interview. It was another groundbreaking broadcast. Michael was a figure of absolute fascination, yet little was actually known about him or how he lived. He so very rarely gave interviews, and although Neverland had become famous, only those lucky enough to be invited inside knew exactly what it was like. That, however, was where the interview took place: Oprah and Michael roamed about the grounds and chatted in the heart of the property, which was classically and elegantly decorated.

But it was the funfair and the emphasis on children that made Neverland such an extraordinary place.

Michael tried to explain it, with reference to his own background and his lost childhood. 'People wonder why I always have children around, because I find the thing that I never had through them – you know, Disneyland, amusement parks, arcade games,' he said. 'I adore all that stuff because when I was little, it was always work, work, work; from one concert to the next. If it wasn't a concert, it was the recording studio; if it wasn't that, it was TV shows or picture sessions. There was always something to do.'

The Jackson family was, in fact, already dogged by scandal that year. La Toya Jackson had published an autobiography, *Growing Up in the Jackson Family*, claiming that she and her sister Maureen 'Rebbie' had been abused by their father Joe when they were children, something Rebbie point-blank denied. Oprah put these allegations to Michael and he firmly, but politely, declined to answer, saying he hadn't read the book and that he loved his sister. At that point, La Toya was estranged from the whole family, but in 1997 she returned to the fold.

Michael spoke at length about his parents, as well. 'I love my father, but I don't know him,' he said. 'Am I angry with him? Sometimes I do get angry. I don't know him the way I'd like to know him. My mother's wonderful. To me, she's perfection. I just wish I could understand my father... I don't know if I was his golden child or whatever, but he was very strict, very hard, very stern – just a look would scare you.'

Michael used the interview to refute a lot of the rumours: that he wanted a white child to play him in the Pepsi commercial ('That is the most ridiculous, horrifying story I've ever heard!'), that he wanted to buy the bones of the Elephant Man and that he bleached his skin (although as previously mentioned, he was deluding himself about that one). As for the plastic surgery, Michael pointed out that if everyone who lived in L.A. who had had plastic surgery moved away, there wouldn't be anyone left in town: 'I think I am right, it would be empty,' he said. In another indication of the torment he was going through, he also added that he tried not to look in the mirror.

They also talked about the pressure that Michael was under: 'When you're on top of the world, when you've broken every record going, just what do you do for an encore?' asked Oprah. 'It makes it harder each time to follow up,' Michael confessed. 'You just try to be as original as you can be without thinking about statistics; you just go from the soul and from the heart.' But now the pressure heaped on him was astounding, and it was about to get worse.

Oprah pressed on with questions that the world really was curious to find out about. Michael declined to answer her question as to whether he was a virgin (the answer, at that stage, was probably yes), but he did admit that he wanted to get married. 'I would feel like my life is incomplete if I do not because I adore the family life,' he said. 'I adore children and I adore that whole thing. And I would love to, that's one of my dreams, but I couldn't right now because I'm married: I'm married to my music and there has to be that closeness in order to do the kind of work that I want to do.'

Elizabeth Taylor, one of the few major stars to continue to support Michael in the ordeal that lay ahead, then came on the show. It was widely acknowledged, even by the most adoring fans, that Michael had a reputation for being a little unusual and she addressed that head-on, too. 'If he has any eccentricities, it's that he is like larger than life and some people just cannot accept that or face it, or understand it,' she explained. 'His talent on stage, why I call him the King of Pop, Rock, Soul, Music, Entertainment, whatever...'

She was also asked if the bond between them was somewhat strange. 'Well, it's not,' was her reply. 'I mean, our childhoods are very similar and we had that from the very beginning in common. I was a child star at 9, had an abusive father, and that kind of brought us together in the very beginning.'

A tour of the estate followed, with Oprah noting that in the theatre, beds had actually been built into the walls to accommodate very sick children on intravenous drips. 'They can't sit up, and these beds, they are hospital beds,' Michael explained. 'You push a button, you go up or you go down, and they are able to watch. We have a magic show, we show the current films, there's cartoons... anything, you know, anything so they can escape to that world of magic that they don't have a chance to experience, the world I was deprived of when I was little.'

There had been a great deal of talk about the unhappiness in his past, but Michael was clear that he had found some peace: by being able to give back. And it is unquestionably true that at that stage, he was doing an enormous amount to help the world's disadvantaged. Apart from all the sick children that he invited to Neverland, there were wider issues too, which he was helping to tackle: 'Heal the World Foundation, which I've formed, which helps children in healing the world,' explained Michael. 'We're doing Heal L.A., which is, we have three primary goals: immunising of children, mentoring a Big Brothers, Big Sisters program, and educating in drug abuse. Jimmy Carter has teamed up with us to do Heal Atlanta and we're going to go from state to state healing – you know, we've gone to Sarajevo, we've done lots of places.'

He attempted to describe another reason why children were so important to him: that unlike just about everyone else he had to deal with, they told the truth. To Oprah's frank incredulity, Michael told her that following Motown 25, which everyone else took, correctly, to be one of the highlights not just of his career, but of popular music in the 1980s, he'd been disappointed by his performance and was in tears about it afterwards until a child comforted him.

'After Motown 25, yes,' he said. 'But then as I was walking to the car, there was this little boy – he was like 12, a little Jewish kid – and he said, "Ooh, you were amazing, who taught you to ever dance like that?" And for the first time I felt like I did a good job. Because I know children don't lie and I just felt so good about it then.' Animals had the same effect on him, too: 'I find in animals the same thing I find so wonderful in children: that purity, that honesty, where they don't judge you; they just want to be your friend. I think that is so sweet.'

Oprah then asked Michael how it felt to be at the centre of such adulation. Only a few performers had experienced the kind of adoration that he had, and anyone who had not been the focus of the screaming crowds, the audiences and everything that Michael had endured for almost his entire life, could hardly begin to imagine what it might be like. 'How,' she asked, 'did it feel?' 'Love,' said Michael. 'You just feel lots of love, and I feel blessed and honoured to be able to be an instrument of nature that was chosen to give them that, what I give them. I'm very honoured and happy about that.' He also felt, '[that] I was chosen as an instrument to just give music and love and harmony to the world. To children of all ages and, um, adults and teenagers.'

Of course, that interview made fascinating viewing. Oprah asked all the questions the world was eager to know about and Michael had, to a certain extent, provided a fair few of the answers. Unwittingly, he had done something else, too: he had spoken at such length about children; his adoration of them and his fascination for them and in so doing he created an Achilles heel for himself. It was impossible to attack Michael on any other grounds because whatever his private addiction to painkillers, he was not openly a drug-user, nor an alcoholic nor indeed a womaniser, so there was very little that anyone could hold against him. Potential enemies included anyone who wanted to extort money from him; for Michael, as the whole world knew, and as evidenced by the tour of Neverland that he gave Oprah, was now exceedingly wealthy.

Michael was on tour in Thailand when the news broke on 24 August 1993: he was accused of child abuse and was under investigation by the Los Angeles Police Department. Several children had been questioned in connection with the charges: Macaulay Culkin, then 12, star of the *Home Alone* films and Michael's video *Black Or White*, and Jordan Chandler, a 13-year-old boy that

Michael befriended the year before. Culkin has always insisted that his relationship with Michael Jackson was nothing more than a totally innocent friendship.

The shock of these allegations and their impact on the public cannot be overestimated. Michael did have particular friends, it was well known among his associates, but paedophilia? That was another matter altogether. However, when mud is flung, particularly as vehemently as it was in this case, some of it sticks – and it did. For Michael, life would never be the same again.

Michael issued an immediate statement through his lawyer Anthony Pellicano, completely denying the allegations. 'I am confident the Police Department will conduct a fair and thorough investigation and that the result will demonstrate that there was no wrongdoing on my part,' it read. Pellicano further added that about 30 attempts to blackmail Michael were made each year and this was, according to him, a $20 million extortion plot. There were signs, though, that Michael's camp underestimated the trouble ahead even though this was not, by a long shot, the first time that anyone had tried to extort money from him.

Certainly, many of those close to Michael were adamant the story couldn't be true. 'He was a Jehovah's Witness,' recounted Stephen Davis, who had written Michael's autobiography, *Moon Walk*. 'In all the time I spent with him, there was never any reference to his sexuality, his feelings for women – or men. I tried to pry, using my sharply honed journalistic skills to figure out with who, or what he was having sex with. I came up with nothing; he was almost otherworldly.'

Others stood up for Michael, including some friends who just happened to be children, too. It was perhaps unfortunate that they confirmed that they had, indeed, shared a bed with him. Brett Barnes, 11, and Wade Robson, 10, both went on television with their mothers to assure the world that nothing was wrong. Both were adamant that Michael himself was nothing more than a big kid (something borne out entirely by many who met him, even briefly); he was someone they enjoyed spending time with in a totally innocent way. Sharing a bed was like a slumber party: 'I was on one side of the bed and he was on the other,' said Brett. 'It was a big bed.'

Macaulay Culkin, one of Michael's best-known young friends and someone else who knew all about the pressures of being a child star, was also adamant that it simply wasn't true. 'I've heard all the stories, but you have to know Michael,' he said, as an adult. 'He's not like anybody else. There's this expression about how somebody's a big kid, it's always just an expression. But with Michael, he is one. We had pillow fights, we goofed around, we rode on the rides, but at the time it just seemed so harmless. Michael is just Michael, and if you really knew him, you would know just how stupid the accusations are.'

As the severity of the situation began to sink in, Michael cancelled two of his scheduled concerts in Bangkok, claiming dehydration. (Coke, Pepsi's great rival, promptly placed a half-page advertisement in all the Bangkok English-speaking newspapers: 'Dehydrated? There's always Coke,' it read.) As the situation looked increasingly grim, Elizabeth Taylor and Janet Jackson both flew to Thailand to be with him.

Matters soon went from bad to worse. While the rest of the family rallied round, La Toya Jackson issued a statement that she would later retract and apologise for, but which caused enormous damage at the time. According to her, she could, 'no longer be a silent collaborator of his crimes against small innocent children,' adding that she, '...hopes he gets help. If I remain silent, then that means that I feel the guilt and humiliation that these children are feeling and I think that is very wrong. Now you stop and you think for one second, and you tell me, what 35-year-old man is going to take a little boy and stay with him for 30 days, and take another boy and stay with him for 5 days in a room and never leave the room?'

It is hard to imagine what La Toya's motives were: it can only be noted that she herself was in a controlling relationship at the time with her then husband, on top of which the Jacksons did have form when it came to that sort of thing. Over the years, there had been various rifts, although they had always been patched up. Not only was Michael the subject of constant press attention, the whole family experienced it, too. Even so, it was an extraordinary intervention to make. If La Toya believed what she was saying, going public and humiliating a brother already deeply damaged by the allegations could hardly help matters.

Nor would Pepsi stand by their man. They were sponsoring Michael's latest tour, but let it be known that when it came to an end, so too did the deal. For nine years now, they had been working together, but their action effectively brought the *Dangerous* tour to a close. Michael had been through Europe, Asia, Australia and Latin America, but the US was not to enjoy the latest venture from its most celebrated son.

With the cancellation of the tour, Michael checked into rehab. His dependence on painkillers had grown to such an extent that family and friends were becoming increasingly concerned. Public opinion, meanwhile, flailed wildly. On the one hand, most people simply could not believe charges that the Peter Pan of pop was something far more sinister: this was *Michael Jackson*, after all, someone who loved children and animals, who wanted to give something back to the world. On the other hand (and particularly in the UK), the media were having a field day: if nothing else, it was a good story, especially as it involved one of the most complex celebrities of all time.

The Los Angeles Police Department moved swiftly and conducted a detailed search of Neverland. When Michael returned to the US, matters became even worse. The boy Jordan had provided police with a description of Michael's genitalia and the police insisted on a strip search. Michael submitted to this in what was to be one of the most humiliating episodes in his life: for all the public display, he was an intensely private man, after all. As it happens, there was no conclusive match with what Jordan said; he claimed Michael was circumcised, whereas this did not prove to be the case.

But Michael himself had finally had enough. Apart from strenuously denying the allegations, he said little in public on the subject, but the story was running out of control. Apart from anything else, there was a real danger that this episode might put paid to his career: for all his protestations about the stress of life in the limelight, this was something he certainly had no wish to see. And so, somewhat belatedly, his advisors decided that the best thing for him to do was to speak directly to the public: they had no desire to filter his words through the medium of an interview because the press had been raising a storm and there was no telling what the result might be.

And so it was that for the second time in a year, the public was invited to Neverland, from where Michael issued a televised statement, which is now repeated here in full. 'Good afternoon,' he began. 'To all my friends and fans, I wish to convey my deepest gratitude for your love and support. I am doing well and I am strong. As you may already know, after my tour ended I remained out of the country undergoing treatment for a dependency on pain medication. This medication was initially prescribed to soothe the excruciating pain that I was suffering after recent reconstructive surgery on my scalp.

'There have been many disgusting statements made recently concerning allegations of improper conduct on my part. These statements about me are totally false. As I have maintained from the very beginning, I am hoping for a speedy end to this horrifying, horrifying experience to which I have been subjected. I shall not in this statement respond to all the false allegations being made against me since my lawyers have advised me that. [sic]

'I will say I am particularly upset by the handling of this matter by the incredible, terrible mass media. At every opportunity, the media has dissected and manipulated these allegations to reach their own conclusions. I ask all of you to wait to hear the truth before you label or condemn me. Don't treat me like a criminal because I am innocent.

'I have been forced to submit to a dehumanizing and

humiliating examination by the Santa Barbara County Sheriff's Department and the Los Angeles Police Department earlier this week. They served a search warrant on me, which allowed them to view and photograph my body, including my penis, my buttocks, my lower torso, thighs and any other areas that they wanted. They were supposedly looking for any discoloration, spotting, blotches or other evidence of a skin color disorder called vitiligo, which I have previously spoken about.

'The warrant also directed me to cooperate in any examination of my body by their physician to determine the condition of my skin, including whether I have vitiligo or any other skin disorder. The warrant further stated that I had no right to refuse the examination or photographs and if I failed to cooperate with them they would introduce that refusal at any trial as an indication of my guilt.

'It was the most humiliating ordeal of my life – one that no person should ever have to suffer. And even after experiencing the indignity of this search, the parties involved were still not satisfied and wanted to take even more pictures. It was a nightmare, a horrifying nightmare. But if this is what I have to endure to prove my innocence, my complete innocence, so be it.

'Throughout my life, I have only tried to help thousands upon thousands of children to live happy lives. It brings tears to my eyes when I see any child who suffers. I am not guilty of these allegations. But if I am guilty of anything it is of giving all that I have to give to help children all over the world. It is of loving children of all ages and races; it is of gaining sheer joy from seeing children with their innocent and smiling faces. It is of enjoying through them the childhood that I missed myself. If I am guilty of anything, it is of believing what God said about children: "Suffer little children to come unto me and forbid them not, for such is the kingdom of heaven." In no way do I think that I am God, but I do try to be godlike in my heart.

'I am totally innocent of any wrongdoing and I know these terrible allegations will all be proven false. Again, to my friends and fans, thank you very much for all of your support. Together we will see this through to the very end. I love you very much and may God bless you all. I love you. Goodbye.'

Up until this point, the public was largely with Michael, viewing Evan Chandler as an opportunist, who saw in his son's admittedly unusual friendship with an extremely famous celebrity the chance to make some money. A poll conducted by *Entertainment Weekly* revealed that only 12 per cent of adults believed the allegations, while the sales of Michael's records were actually on the rise. But then he made the biggest mistake of his life.

It has never been entirely clear why Michael agreed to a pay-off. According to his biographer, J. Randy Taraborrelli, Chandler's lawyer petitioned the court to be allowed access to the star's finances, saying that his fortune would give him an advantage in court. For Michael, this was enough. For his body to be examined was one thing, but to have strangers start sifting through his finances was something else.

Another possibility is that he simply wanted the case to go away. It is easy to forget that Michael never, at any stage, lived a normal life; he had no idea what that might be. Even those other two greats of the eighties, Prince and Madonna, experienced everyday life when they were growing up and for all the wealth that they went on to accumulate, they understood what it was to be an ordinary Joe.

But Michael's strange childhood, combined with an adulthood spent totally isolated from anything normal in the rest of the world, meant that he simply didn't understand how society operated. A decade on, the fact came sharply into focus once more when he told TV journalist Martin Bashir that he shared his bed with children, but it also meant that he didn't understand quite how bad something might look and as a man of such enormous wealth, he was accustomed to paying his way out of problems. Given the case had been dragging on for nearly six months now, he really wanted it to go away.

And so, in late January 1994, he settled the civil suit for $22 million, which he paid to Jordan, his mother June and lawyer Larry Feldman. The civil charge was dropped, and as there was no evidence against him, the police dropped criminal charges as well. Everyone involved in the case signed a legal document saying they wouldn't talk about it; Michael and Jordan Chandler never spoke again.

Asked why he'd done it, Michael replied, 'I wanted to go on with my life. Too many people had already been hurt. I want to make records, I want to sing; I want to perform again... It's my talent, my hard work, my life, my decision.'

But it turned out to be a terrible choice. Although the public had been largely supportive, the mood changed sharply, with some questioning openly why Michael had paid out such a huge sum if he'd done nothing wrong. It made it look as if he had, after all, had something to hide, and that he'd paid out a lot of money to cover up his guilt. For the rest of his life, he had to put up with suggestions that his love of children was sinister, not well meaning at all. From here on, life would never be the same.

In 1999, Evan Chandler attempted to claim $60 million from Michael on the grounds that he'd breached an agreement not to talk: this time the case was thrown out of court.

After this disturbing episode, Michael became noticeably more reserved – a wounded man, wounded still further. At times, he really did seem a little too frail for this world, and this was one such circumstance.

But something totally unexpected arose from the affair, too. During the course of events of the previous few months, Michael had reestablished contact with an old childhood friend. He had poured out his heart to her, and she, in turn, had offered him moral support. Given her background, she knew exactly what it was like to live in the full heat of the limelight; she understood what pressures and dangers overwhelming celebrity could bring. At one of the most difficult times of his life, she offered rare succor to Michael and gave him some comfort in his darkest days. Her name was Lisa Marie Presley, and she was shortly to become his first wife.

CHAPTER TEN

A MARRIAGE OF DYNASTIES

At first, no one could believe the news. Michael Jackson and Lisa Marie Presley? *Married*? It couldn't possibly be true. But it was: Michael and Lisa Marie were married on 26 May 1994 at the chic Casa de Campo resort in the Dominican Republic. The King of Pop had wed the daughter of the King of Rock and Roll. For that reason alone, it was a match that captured the world's imagination.

In actual fact, the couple initially met nearly two decades earlier, when both were youngsters, at the MGM Grand Hotel and Casino, when Lisa Marie, aged seven, had attended some of the Jackson 5 shows. And it was by no means as unusual a pairing as it first looked. While Lisa Marie was nowhere near as famous as Michael, her father certainly had been, which meant that she was one of the few people he knew well, who really did know what it was like to be in the spotlight. And unlike his other confidantes, the Liz Taylors and Diana Rosses, Lisa Marie, then 26, was the right age for him. She herself had previously been married: to Danny Keough, whom she wed aged 20. The couple had two children, Danielle Riley and Benjamin Storm. In May 1994, 12 days before her marriage to Michael, Lisa Marie divorced her first husband. Michael had initially mentioned marriage on the phone, apparently asking her, 'If I asked you to marry me, would you do it?' The answer was yes.

Even so, the world was amazed, and so Michael and Lisa Marie went on the Diane Sawyer show to explain that, yes, this was a real relationship. There had been a great deal of cynicism about it in the press, with claims that Michael married Lisa Marie to improve his image, while Lisa Marie married Michael to launch a singing career. In actual fact, theirs was a real relationship, albeit a short-lived one, and it did have a sexual side.

Diane asked Michael how it came about and Michael explained that he had tried to get something started with Lisa Marie via his lawyer, John Branca, but nothing was forthcoming. Eventually, when Michael found out that Lisa Marie had got married, he was very upset and jealous. When they finally did get together, in the wake of Lisa Marie's separation from her first husband,

Michael proposed after just four months, and over the telephone. 'Yeah, anyway, we were spending a lot of time together,' said Lisa. 'I don't know how it didn't manage to get in the press, because we weren't hiding it. I was in Las Vegas, we were in… everywhere.'

The pair confirmed that a pre-nuptial agreement had been signed.

Naturally, the conversation turned to the Jordan Chandler accusations. Michael insisted the contact between himself and the boy had not been of a sexual nature, that he never sexually engaged with him or fondled him in any way – harming a child was just not in his nature, he stated.

'And what do you think should be done to someone who does that?' Diane asked.

'What I think should be *done*? Gee… I think they need help in some kind of way,' was his reply.

The question on everyone's lips was, of course, why he had chosen to settle out of court rather than clear his name in front of a jury. To many, this action could have been taken as an indication of guilt, that he did have something to hide and that there were things he did not want to come out in the public arena of a courthouse. On the advice of his people, he had elected to settle in the hope of concluding the whole matter swiftly.

'It was hands-down, a unanimous decision – resolve

the case. This could be something that could go on for seven years,' he explained.

He was also very keen to point out that at no time had anyone found anything that might implicate him. 'There wasn't one piece of information that says I did this. And anyway, they turned my room upside down, went through all my books, all my videotapes, all my private things and they found nothing, nothing, nothing; nothing that could say Michael Jackson did this. Nothing!'

Then there was his habit of sharing a bed with young boys, also a tricky area.

'...I'll be happy to answer it. I have never invited anyone into my bed, ever. Children love me, I love them; they follow me, they want to be with me. But... anybody can come in my bed, a child can come in my bed, if they want.'

Lisa Marie confirmed that the kids at Neverland would not leave Michael alone and followed him wherever he went. Michael went on to reiterate that the sleepovers were innocent in their nature, with nothing untoward about them.

With that, a pre-recorded clip of an interview with Elizabeth Taylor was shown, and she, too, spoke of her belief that Michael would never harm a child. 'When he's on tour, he goes to hospitals without the press following him,' she said. 'Without anyone knowing, he'll get up in a disguise and do it. [He'll] take his disguise off when he's there and kids know, "Wow! It's Michael Jackson!"'

Did she, Elizabeth, suspect for a moment that something was wrong? 'No way!' she stated firmly. 'Absolutely not! I know Michael's heart; I know his mind and his soul. I'm not that insensitive, especially to him, or people I love.'

In a rather eerie foreshadowing of what would happen in the wake of the child abuse trial of 2005, Diane then asked Michael if he was thinking of moving abroad and he confirmed that he had no great desire to stay in the USA any longer, even though Neverland would always belong to him. Perhaps South Africa or Switzerland would suit him better, he added.

Lisa butted in at this point. She wanted to refute another of the numerous rumours swirling around them; that they weren't actually living together. They were.

A clip was shown of the wedding before Diane turned to another of the stories doing the rounds. Lisa Marie's first husband was a Scientologist: it was said that she had become one too and was trying to get her hands on Michael's money to put it into the Church. Given that, courtesy of her surname, Lisa Marie's wealth might well have rivalled that of Michael's, this did seem a little far-fetched. She certainly thought so.

As for Michael himself, Lisa went on, 'Oooh, um...

what do I love the most about him? Everything! Uh, he's amazing. I really admire him. I respect him. I'm in love with him. And no, we don't sleep in separate bedrooms, thank you very much. And I love everything about him.'

Diane then embarked on a rather delicate area – did the couple have sex? To this question, a straight answer was never really given though they did hint that they were planning to have children.

Lisa Marie then cut to the chase. 'Did we marry out of convenience?' she asked. 'That's really interesting to me... Well, why wouldn't we have a lot in common? That's the question. Why? Why not? But you can't live with someone [if it's a fake]. We're together all the time, first of all. Second thing, how can you fake that 24 hours a day with somebody? Sleeping with somebody, waking up with somebody... He's running around the house, I'm running around the house. You were in our house. We have a normal house...'

There was another rumour, too: that they were thinking about adoption. Michael expressed a desire to adopt children of all colours and creeds, but when asked about him adopting Lisa Marie's kids, his new wife was emphatic that they already had a father and that for another man to go about adopting them was simply not right.

Having got to grips with so many controversies surrounding him, including his new album, Diane returned to the subject that seemed to fascinate so many people: Michael's colour.

'Somehow people still are not... they don't feel they've heard everything about the whiteness of your skin, and that it's somehow not a choice on your part...'

'I think it creates itself... nature,' replied Michael calmly.

'He's... he's an artist. He has every right. And he is constantly re-modifying something, or changing it, or reconstructing it or, you know, working on some imperfection he thinks needs to be worked on,' insisted Lisa Marie. 'If he sees something he doesn't like, he changes it. Period. He re-sculptured himself, he's an artist.'

For a while, the relationship continued. While speculation never ceased about the reality behind it all, the couple certainly attempted to prove the doubters wrong: they made an appearance at the 1994 MTV Video Music Awards, something the *New York Times* called a 'surprise coup.' 'And think, nobody thought this would last,' said Michael to the audience, before turning to Lisa and giving her a passionate embrace. The crowd went ballistic: this was the only time Michael had ever been seen in a clinch in his life. Lisa was also with him during the making of the next album and yet another hugely controversial video. At one stage, when she was seen on set, she appeared to be advising him. Why not? She knew the business too.

In the event, the marriage was not to last: the couple divorced after just two years, with some reports insisting that Michael wanted to start a family, while Lisa Marie did not. There were also allegations that he'd been neglecting her, but then Michael didn't really know any other way to live. Public property for all his life, he had never had to take the needs of another into account. Really, he wasn't capable of maintaining the kind of close relationship that Lisa so clearly wanted. Of course, the newspapers had a field day with, 'She's Out Of His Life'-style headlines, but the couple did stay in touch and Lisa was always adamant that the child abuse allegations simply were not true. As she pointed out on one occasion, she had children herself and would never have stayed with a man she thought capable of such actions.

Meanwhile, Michael's career, expected in some quarters to be derailed by the child abuse allegations, was actually coming back on track. Although his record sales were never quite going to match what they once had been, nonetheless he was far from finished and was still showing a good deal of the financial acumen that had stood him in such good stead in his youth. In 1995, he merged his Northern Songs catalogue with Sony's publishing division, creating a new entity, Sony/ATV Music Publishing, something he maintained a stake in right up to the time of his death. This deal earned him

$95 million and also provided him with an income from more songs, including, appropriately, Elvis numbers.

There was also something defiant about the launch of the next album, *HIStory*. Over the last few years, Michael had been through the mill and back, something that was to be reflected in some of the songs on the record, but he was clearly intent on showing that, when it came down to it, no one could make pop music like he could. And whatever else he'd been through, it still holds true today.

HIStory: Past, Present and Future, Book 1 was a double album. The first disc contained 15 greatest hits, the second, new material. There was a very different feel about this album: it was full of barely concealed fury, something Michael had never shown in his music before. A lot was riding on it, too. It was released in June 1995, the first album release since *Dangerous* four years previously. Since then, of course, there had been the abuse allegations: it was in everyone's interest to make sure it went well.

Sony asked Michael how he would like the launch to proceed. 'Build a statue of me,' he replied, and they did. 'It was a brilliant idea, but I hope it doesn't catch on,' quipped one Sony executive. 'We've got a lot of four- and five-piece bands. It could get expensive!'

In fact, the launch of the album alone was said to have cost around $30 million, with Sony clearly determined to protect its biggest star. The 30ft-high steel-truss fibreglass structure was created by Derek Haworth, who was a sculptor based in Hertfordshire. In the event, nine more sculptures were dotted across Europe, with the London-based statue floated down the Thames and moored at the Tower of London for a week before being taken on a tour around the UK.

What really set the cat among the pigeons, though, was the short film that Michael made as a teaser for the album. Whatever you might think of the content, this was an astonishing piece of work: shots of thousands of soldiers marching in formation through the streets interspersed with men at work in steel factories. At the head of the soldiers marched Michael, with the crowd screaming in adoration. Helicopters buzzed around a giant statue of the hero of the hour. Directed by Rupert Wainwright, it was filmed in Hungary and, on its release, compared to the Nazi propaganda film *Triumph of the Will*, directed by Leni Riefenstahl. Given that Michael was accused of anti-Semitism in another of the songs on the album, this was pretty hot stuff.

When it was put to him that the film had Nazi overtones, Michael point-blank denied this was his intention. What he and Sony wanted to do, however, was to drum up attention and they certainly managed that. In the interview with Diane Sawyer, Michael insisted the film had no political overtones, but he did admit that he had hoped it might stir up controversy and get people talking.

'Yeah!' said Michael. 'They fell into my trap. I wanted everybody's attention. No, the symbols have nothing to do with that. It's not political, it's not fascist; it's not dogma. It's not, you know, ideology and all this stuff. It's pure, simple love. You don't see any tanks, you don't see any cannons: it's about love, it's people coming together.' In fact, this was rather disingenuous, for it was also about helicopters firing on people. But Michael was an old pro: he knew exactly what he was doing and if he wanted to get attention, it worked.

Then there were the lyrics of 'They Don't Care About Us'. This time, Michael found himself in real trouble and had allegations of anti-Semitism thrown at him. He was subsequently forced to issue various apologies and alter the wording of the song. Cue uproar.

The *New York Times* got hold of a copy of the lyrics before the record was officially released and accused Michael of anti-Semitism. He responded by issuing a statement that dealt with the accusation head-on. 'The idea that these lyrics could be deemed objectionable is extremely hurtful to me, and misleading,' he said. 'The song in fact is about the pain of prejudice and hate, and is a way to draw attention to social and political problems. I am the voice of the accused and the attacked. I am the voice of everyone. I am the skinhead,

I am the Jew; I am the black man, I am the white man. I am not the one who was attacking. It is about the injustices to young people and how the system can wrongfully accuse them. I am angry and outraged that I could be so misinterpreted.'

The anti-Semitic accusations levelled at him as a result of those lyrics came up in the Diane Sawyer interview as well.

'It's not anti-Semitic because I'm not a racist,' said Michael fiercely. 'I could never be a racist. I love all races of people, from Arabs to Jewish people... like I said before, to blacks. But when I say, "Jew me, sue me, everybody do me, kick me, kike me, don't you black or white me", I'm talking about myself as the victim, you know. My accountants and lawyers are Jewish. My best friends are Jewish... David Geffen, Jeffrey Katzenberg, Steven Spielberg, Mike Milkin. These are friends of mine. They're all Jewish. So how does that make sense? I was raised in a Jewish community.'

Michael's manager, Sandy Gallin, leapt to his defence. 'When I heard those lyrics, I thought they were brilliant,' he said. 'He's saying, stop labelling people, stop degrading people, stop calling them names. The song is about not being prejudiced. To take two lines out of context is unfair.'

But the furore refused to die down and so Michael wrote to Rabbis Marvin Hier and Abraham Cooper, dean and associate dean of the Simon Wiesenthal Center, apologising once more. 'Unfortunately, my choice of words may have unintentionally hurt the very people I wanted to stand in solidarity with. I just want you all to know how strongly I am committed to tolerance, peace and love, and I apologize to anyone who might have been hurt,' he said. However, there were plans to include the apology in future editions of the album.

Rabbi Hier believed this was a genuine mistake. 'I do not think Michael Jackson is an anti-Semite,' he said. 'I've known Michael. I took him around the Museum of Tolerance, an exhibition at the Wiesenthal Center on racism in the United States and on the Holocaust. He was emotionally overcome, he cried. We will follow this up. If they do not put this disclaimer on, then we will say they did not honour the agreement.'

Ultimately, the lyrics were deemed to have gone just too far and Michael changed them for future editions of the record. Even the accompanying video, directed by Spike Lee, raised eyebrows – or rather, the *two* accompanying videos, for the original took place in a prison and showed scenes of violence, which provoked MTV into taking it off its playlist. An alternative had already been shot in Dona Marta, a shanty town in Brazil, and this was eventually the version that went out.

But that certainly wasn't the end of it. One of the singles from the album was 'You Are Not Alone', featuring Lisa Marie. This one raised eyebrows because Michael appeared nearly naked in the video. Then there was 'Scream', his duet with his sister Janet, and the first single to be released. It was a bellow of rage at the newspaper coverage of the Jordan Chandler business, and in some ways a video sequel to 1989's 'Leave Me Alone'. Even Michael, it seemed, was beginning to feel that finally, he had had enough. The accompanying video, featuring Michael and Janet in a spaceship, was deemed one of the best he had ever made. But there were other furious sallies, too: 'Tabloid Junkie' was another attack on the press, as was 'This Time Around'.

However, Michael's other concerns featured on the album too, most notably in the third single to come from it: 'Earth Song'. Talking about exactly that, the future of the planet, 'Earth Song' was to be one of his later signature tunes. It became Michael's best-selling single in the UK, where it debuted at No. 1 and went on to sell over a million copies. It was the Christmas No. 1 that year too, keeping the first Beatles single for 25 years, 'Free As A Bird', off the top slot.

There was a slightly unfortunate addendum to all this: Michael sang the song at the 1996 Brit Awards, which he also attended to receive the Artist Of A Generation award. As he was performing, a drunken Jarvis Cocker disgraced himself by jumping on the stage and mooning at the audience before being removed by security guards.

There were also signs that stress really was beginning to take its toll. From the *Thriller* days onwards, Michael had become accustomed to controversy, but now it was getting all too much. 1993 had been a dreadful year for him, with the child abuse allegations, and this was followed in 1994 by the charge that his marriage to Lisa Marie was not a real one. Then the *HIStory* album, while certainly bringing him the attention he craved, was mired in controversy wherever he looked. Towards the end of 1995, he collapsed during rehearsals for a TV special: the cause, ominously – given the number of painkillers, anti-anxiety drugs and anti-depressants he would go on to consume – was stress.

But still Michael battled on. He was a pro and *HIStory* did well. The reviews were, on the whole, positive. 'Some of the new songs – the excellent current single "Scream" or the first-rate R&B ballad "You Are Not Alone" – manage to link the incidents of Jackson's infamous recent past to universal concepts like injustice or isolation,' wrote James Hunter in *Rolling Stone*. 'When he bases his music in the bluntness of hip-hop, Jackson sketches funky scenarios denouncing greed, blanket unreliability and false accusation. *HIStory* unfolds in Jackson's outraged response to everything he has encountered in the last year or so.'

The album went on to receive five Grammy Award nominations and in the event, it won one: Best Video,

Short Form for 'Scream'. Although sales didn't quite match his previous triumphs, Michael was still breaking records with ease. *HIStory* is, to this day, the best-selling multiple-disc album ever, with sales of 20 million, and it proved beyond a shadow of a doubt that Michael Jackson was still a force to be reckoned with in the music industry. The accompanying tour was also a huge success: Michael remained a massively popular performer, whatever his recent travails, and he played to more than 4.5 million fans in 58 cities, in 35 countries. This was a performer who could still pull the audiences in a big way when he tried.

Meanwhile, his thoughts were turning elsewhere. Although this was by no means the end of his musical career, he simply didn't have anything left to prove anymore, hadn't done so for years. What he was thinking about now was a family. Michael's love of children was real all right but for years, he had been spending time with other people's kids. Now, in his late thirties, he was beginning to realise something: he wanted a family of his own – and he wanted one now.

CHAPTER ELEVEN
A FAMILY MAN

The news, when it filtered through, was almost as surprising as it had been first time around when the union with Lisa Marie Presley came out: Michael had married again. This time it was to Debbie Rowe, who worked as a nurse for Michael's dermatologist, Dr. Arnold Klein. The wedding took place on 15 November 1996, at the Sheraton Hotel in Sydney, Australia, when Michael was on the *HIStory* tour. He was 38, while she was 37 and six months pregnant with his first child.

Debbie and Michael had actually met years previously, when he came to an appointment with Dr. Klein. 'I go "Hi". And he goes "Hi," and I said, "You know what? Nobody does what you do better, and nobody does what I do better. Let's get this over with." And he laughed, and we just became friends. It was just right away,' Debbie later revealed.

The two became genuine buddies. According to Debbie: 'He'd call and say, "Hi, what are you doing? Do you want to get a video?" We'd sneak out without security. We got caught. I thought, "Oh my God, this is like a Beatles film! We're getting chased by people."'

The idea that they might have a child together came about in the wake of the breakdown of Michael's marriage to Lisa Marie. It might have been an unconventional union, but he was genuinely saddened by the collapse, not least because he so badly wanted a family of his own. 'I was trying to console him, because he was really upset,' said Debbie. 'He was upset because he really wanted to be a dad. I said, "So, be a dad." He looked at me, puzzled. That is when I looked at him and said, "Let me do this, I want to do this. You have been so good to me; you are such a great friend. Please let me do this. You need to be a dad, and I want you to be." I believe there are people who should be parents, and he's one of them. And he is such a fabulous man, and such a good friend, and he's always been there for me, always, from the day I met him.'

Debbie was already six months pregnant by the time they got married, and she has said the marriage took place to avoid the stigma of illegitimacy. 'To prevent some of the taboo of a child out of wedlock,' she

Above: Michael with his sisters, La Toya and Janet, at his trial in 2004.

Below left: Fans stand by their beloved King of Pop.

Below right: Michael was acquitted on all counts of child molestation at the end of his trial.

Above: Performing at the 'United We Stand: What More Can I Give?' concert, in remembrance of September 11.

Below: Addressing some of the controversy surrounding him on Reverend Al Sharpton's radio show.

On 15th November 2006, Michael received a Diamond Award at the World
Music Awards for selling over 100 million albums.

Above: Performing at the ceremony.

Below: Beyoncé Knowles presents him with his statuette.

The wait is over. Michael announces his Summer 2009 residency at the O2 Arena in London. Tickets for the concerts sold out in a matter of hours.

Above: A Michael Jackson lookalike is surrounded by fans outside the O2 Arena.

Below: Michael's last rehearsal for the highly anticipated 'This Is It' tour.

© *Getty Images.*

News of Michael Jackson's death on 25 June 2009 sent shockwaves of devastation and disbelief throughout the world, and the tributes came pouring in.

Above: The Michael Jackson public memorial service was held on 7 July 2009 at the Staples Center in Los Angeles, where Michael had been rehearsing for his forthcoming tour.

Below: Flowers and tributes were left on Michael's star on the Walk of Fame.

R.I.P. Michael Jackson. 29 August 1958 – 25 June 2009.

explained. 'The kids were going to have it hard enough as it was, and they didn't need to have that label upon them, like their father has had so many placed upon him; they shouldn't.'

When Debbie actually came to give birth, Michael was beside himself. 'We were very excited,' she recalled. 'Michael was definitely more excited than I was. He was so excited when we had a contraction, and he was there. We had videos and music. But he was there the whole time: held my hand, stroked my head. I had a very "colourful" language, and every time I went to say something, Michael would cut me off with words like "shoot" and "fudge." He didn't like curses; he didn't think it was necessary when other words would do.'

In fact, Debbie was impregnated by artificial insemination and in the wake of Michael's death she went on to claim that he was not the biological father of the two children she bore him. That, actually, is unimportant. Michael was to be their father in every other sense of the world, utterly doting on his offspring, the kids he had wanted so badly for so many years. On 13 February 1997, back in Los Angeles, Debbie gave birth. 'I'd never seen Michael so happy and that's what made it so wonderful for me,' she said.

The baby was born in a hospital, but shortly afterwards taken to Neverland. Meanwhile, the paparazzi had gone into a feeding frenzy as never before. The King of Pop, music's Peter Pan, the young boy who had never grown up, was now, at long last, a father himself. It seemed only yesterday that Michael was the bright-eyed, bushy-tailed 11-year-old prancing about on stage, but here he was, approaching 40, finally a family man.

Fatherhood brought Michael a kind of peace he would never attain elsewhere. For a start, as with most fathers, he received the unconditional love of his children from the word go. They were the only ones that he could be positive loved him for himself, not for his fame and fortune plus the whole palaver of being Michael Jackson. Bringing them up gave new meaning to his life. Already, he had accomplished more professionally than most people ever manage in several lifetimes, but having a family of his own to look after, rather than the innumerable children he befriended, brought him great joy.

Michael was also an extremely hands-on father. Although a team of nannies were on hand, day and night, to ensure the children were properly cared for, he too did his share of nappy changing, and was known to clear up after them if they made a mess. The children adored him, as witnessed by his daughter Paris's grief-stricken tribute at his funeral. In his kids, Michael found the happiness denied him elsewhere.

The level of media attention was so intrusive that Michael decided to go down the route taken by so many celebrities: to pose for pictures and an interview in the hope that, their interest sated, the press would finally go away. Of course, their hunger was never to be abated: this was Michael Jackson, after all, an object of boundless fascination to the whole world, not just its press.

'I took pictures of the baby,' he told TV journalist Barbara Walters. 'I said, "They're forcing me to get his pictures." There's helicopters flying above us, flying over my house, flying over the hospital, machines and satellites all over. Even the hospital said, "Michael, we've had every kind of celebrity here, but we've never had it like this. This is unbelievable."

'And so I said, "Here, take it." And I gave the money to charity. And now they want to do it again, and I don't want, maybe I don't want to show him to the world like that. I want him to have some space, where he can go to school. I don't want him to be called "Wacko Jacko", that's not nice. They call the father that. That isn't nice, right?'

But the interview he and Debbie gave to *OK!* magazine was very revealing. Asked about the birth, he replied, 'It's hard to take step by step, but the snapshots in my mind from the birth show our excitement and nervousness. Debbie was so strong throughout the delivery. There were shouts of joy when the baby was born. I couldn't believe the miracle I had witnessed. It was unbelievable.'

He was also asked to describe their relationship. 'Debbie and I love each other for all the reasons you will never see on stage or in pictures,' said Michael. 'I fell for the beautiful, unpretentious, giving person that she is, and she fell for me, just being me.'

'I love him even more now than before our son was born,' Debbie added. 'Fatherhood has brought out a very protective streak in him. He is so loving and strong.'

What really happened, of course, is that Debbie had seen how much Michael wanted to be a father and offered to bear him a child. The two had known each other for years, through her work, and in Debbie, Michael knew he had found someone who could do what he wanted – namely, bear his children, but allow him to bring them up alone. They never lived together, although she was also to give him the daughter he craved.

Michael was eager to explain why he named his son as he did. 'His name is Prince Michael Junior,' he explained. 'My grandfather and great-grandfather were both named Prince, so we have carried on that tradition, and now we have a third Prince in the family... Words can't describe it [fatherhood]. There is no miracle in life that compares with watching your son come into the world. He smiles all the time and his eyes twinkle when I sing to him; he definitely knows my voice. Debbie tickles his chin and he giggles.'

Debbie was also keen to explain that Michael was an exceedingly hands-on father. 'Michael does everything,' she said. 'He loves being involved in every aspect of caring for the baby. He is such a wonderful father, feeding him, holding him and, of course, singing to him.'

Michael was determined that Prince Michael's upbringing would be very different from his own. There was to be none of the discipline enforced by Joe: this was a child who was to grow up knowing he was loved and not expected to be the family's main breadwinner. 'I want him to grow up being surrounded by love and family, to receive the best education I can provide him with, to discover and develop his talents, and to use his resources to make life better for those less fortunate than he,' said Michael.

'He's very patient and protective,' Debbie added. 'He never rushes what he's doing with the baby. I was very proud of how tough he was about our privacy. He's incredibly strong.'

Michael was, however, beginning to show signs that he was fed up of the circus that his life had become. He was never able to escape the paparazzi and while, admittedly, his habits, such as appearing masked in public, were a little eccentric, he wanted to draw a line between what was public and what was private. But this was Michael Jackson and whatever he did would never be enough to satisfy a public always desperate to know more.

Barbara Walters put it to him that he didn't help himself with the varying eccentricities. 'There's no mysterious behaviour,' said Michael firmly. 'There's a time, when I give a concert, I like to have as many people who would like to come can come and enjoy the show. And there's a time when you like to be in private, when you put on your pyjamas and go to sleep, cut the light and you lay down, that's your private space. You go to the park. I can't go in the park, so I create my own park at Neverland, my own water space, my movie theatre, my theme park, that's all for me to enjoy.'

And now it was for his children to enjoy, too. The following year, on 3 April 1998, Paris Michael Katherine Jackson was born. It was another case of artificial insemination, this time in Paris, hence the name – 'Michael wanted to call her Princess, but I thought that was stupid,' said Debbie. The child's second middle name, of course, was after Michael's beloved mother. This time, he was so desperate to get his new child home that he later admitted that he cut the cord himself and left while the baby was still covered in blood.

This was a very difficult birth and left Debbie unable to have any more children, something both parents found very distressing. However, Michael did provide properly for the mother of his kids. 'You know what Michael did?' said Debbie. 'He got me the most fabulous place to live! If you read the tabloids, it's the enclave of the enclave, Beverly Hills, which I have no idea what an enclave is, if it's chic-chic, it's cool – I don't know. It's got a wonderful, beautiful yard, a place for my dogs to run, and safe. And I went home, I recovered in my new home.'

About six months after the birth of Paris, knowing she couldn't give Michael any more children, Debbie filed for divorce and received a settlement worth about £4.2 million. In return, she relinquished custodial rights to the children, but claimed her relationship with Michael remained fine. 'It always has been,' she said in 2008. 'Michael and I have always got on. I only divorced him because I wanted my life back; I couldn't cope with the constant pressure of fame. He's the genius, the famous one, not me. I turned out two good-looking kids, but I can't sing, I can't dance.'

As she admitted, she also found the pressures of living on Planet Michael too much. For a very brief period, her marriage made her almost as much a subject of curiosity as her husband: 'I used to be an extrovert, but my marriage made me introverted,' she revealed. 'I was followed everywhere. I hated the fame. After I married Michael, it was hard to keep working. Staff at the clinic sold stories about me to the media. People were offered a million dollars for a picture of me pregnant. I even told my family to sell one – I thought they could do with the money. But they refused.'

In 2001, Debbie actually went to court herself to relinquish all parental rights. 'I did it for him to become a father, not for me to become a mother,' she explained. 'You earn the title "parent". I have done absolutely nothing to earn that title.'

Eventually, Debbie was to end up breeding horses about 60 miles outside of LA, although she suddenly rediscovered her maternal side and expressed an interest in looking after the children in the wake of Michael's death.

With a father like Michael, the children were never going to have a conventional childhood and so this proved to be. Nannies watched over them, day and night. The kids were home schooled at Neverland. Michael arranged for a classroom to be built, where they could be tutored in seclusion. In public, like their father, they always wore masks, something that was Debbie's idea, not Michael's. And while he was roundly criticised for this in some quarters, it was actually a perfectly sensible thing to do. No photographs of them without their masks were published until about 2008, with the result that if they were out and about without their famous father, they didn't need to wear them, given that no one could identify them. And given the very real threat of kidnap, where a fortune like Michael's was involved, going to great lengths to conceal their identity was not so strange as it might at first seem.

On 21 February 2002, the latest addition to the family was Prince Michael Jackson II, known simply as 'Blanket', as it implied soothing someone with love. It is not known who Blanket's biological parents are: indeed, it's thought that Michael didn't know, and nor did the mother who gave birth to the child realise who would become his father.

Blanket became the subject of a notorious incident in November that year, when Michael went to Berlin to accept a lifetime Bambi entertainment award for his work on behalf of children. Staying at the city's Adlon Hotel, he got seemingly carried away and, coming to his fourth-floor balcony, held the child aloft over the rail to show to his fans. He was roundly condemned for this action, and indeed, issued a fulsome apology shortly afterwards, calling it a terrible mistake.

'I offer no excuses for what happened,' he said. 'I got caught up in the excitement of the moment. I would never intentionally endanger the lives of my children.' There were also theories that by this time he was so dependent on prescription drugs that he was incapable of knowing what he was doing. But what is clear is that Michael Jackson doted on his children and was eager for them to enjoy very different life to the one he himself had been forced to endure.

Meanwhile, Michael's career was still doing well. In 1997, he released *Blood On The Dance Floor: HIStory in the Mix*, which contained five new songs, five remixed hits from *HIStory* and went on to become the world's best-selling remix album ever. He was, however, becoming more reclusive these days, preferring to spend time out of the public eye with his children.

At the same time, a bitter – and very public – row with the head of Sony Music, Tommy Mottola, ensued. Their lengthy and exceedingly profitable relationship was no more, with Michael ultimately leaving the label.

The background to all this was the release of Michael's latest – and final – album, *Invincible*. It didn't do anything like as well as its predecessors, leading to dark and unfounded rumours that Sony was quite deliberately undermining Michael's career so that he would fall into debt and be forced to sell his share in their giant music back catalogue back to them. Michael, unused to anything other than spectacular success each time he released an album, took this incredibly badly: he led 200 fans to Sony's Madison Avenue headquarters for a demonstration.

Invincible was released in October 2001, alongside a 30th anniversary celebration of Michael's 30 years in show business at Madison Square Garden, during which he appeared alongside his brothers for the very first time since 1984. Meanwhile, *Invincible* went on to sell 10 million copies worldwide and produced three singles, 'You Rock My World', 'Cry' and 'Butterflies', as well as debuting at the top of the charts in ... different countries. But Michael was used to his albu... massively more than this: what would have ... groundbreaking performance for most entertainers ... actually a disappointment for him.

By then, his profile was much lower and so it came to be that he took another truly dreadful decision that was to impact terribly on his life. In hindsight, it seems clear that his judgment, along with his business acumen (though never his talent) was failing him in his last years: Michael, so cushioned from the realities of most people's lives, not only lived in a way that raised eyebrows, but allowed the spotlight to be pointed on his lifestyle, too.

In the early years of the new millennium, he granted the TV journalist Martin Bashir unprecedented access to himself, Neverland, his children (although they only ever appeared masked) and his life. There was a reason for his choice of interviewer. Michael had known and liked Princess Diana – indeed, he had been grief-stricken to learn of her death – and it was Martin Bashir to whom Diana had famously granted an interview in 1995. His handling of her had been extremely sympathetic and a marked advance in her very public battle with her husband, putting the vast majority of the British public on her side. Clearly, Michael hoped that Bashir would do something similar for him: stories about his eccentricity continued to litter the media and he was tired of this. He wanted to prove to the public that there was nothing wrong with his lifestyle and he was not so odd as he sometimes seemed.

In the light of what was to come, Michael's fans (and Michael himself) felt that he had been betrayed. Bashir obviously had an agenda right from the outset. There was so much he could have asked him – about where his ability to dance came from, for example – whereas instead, he chose to focus on Michael's relationship with children. It was an easy target, given the previous allegations of child abuse.

It was actually Michael's friend Uri Geller who brought the two together: 'Michael liked Martin and he was happy to have him around,' said Uri. 'I said to him, "Michael, maybe it's time to open up to the world."'

In fact, Martin Bashir spent eight months with Michael, from May 2002 to January 2003, telling him that the broadcast would show the real him to the world, with nothing off-limits. Michael didn't appear to have a clue what was going to happen: the only time he showed any discomfort was when the subject of his plastic surgery was brought up. Otherwise, he was open and happy to cooperate.

The documentary started with a tour around Neverland, after which Michael talked openly about the difficulties he had suffered as a child. His father would watch rehearsals with a belt in his hand, he recalled, and would use this if anyone put a foot out of p[...] mentioned that he never struck his own child[...] knew only too well the damage – and not just ph[...] that it would cause.

As the action switched to the Four Seasons Hotel in Las Vegas, Michael recalled more about his life as a child: being forced to be in the same room as his brothers when they were with their groupies and quaking with fear when propositioned by Tatum O'Neal. That he was prepared to discuss such matters so openly was a clear sign that Michael trusted Bashir, but far worse was to follow. After filming the trip to Berlin, during which the Blanket episode happened, and repeatedly avoiding questions about his appearance, they returned to Neverland, where Michael allowed himself to be led into the very dangerous area of talking about his relationships with children.

Despite the fiasco of the previous decade, when he paid off Jordan Chandler, Michael told Bashir that he allowed children to sleep in his bed, while he had the floor. Gavin Arvizo was interviewed for the documentary: he said that Michael helped him beat cancer. While Michael had not shared a bed with Gavin, he continued, he had done so with Macaulay Culkin and his brother Kieran when they were 12 and 10. Michael admitted that he had 'slept in a bed with many children. It's not sexual; we're going to sleep. I tuck them in… it's very charming, it's very sweet.'

And so it went on, as Michael was led deeper and deeper into the mire, saying that he got his inspiration from children, that it was all perfectly natural and hotly denying a sexual element to any of it. Michael didn't think he was doing wrong, so why would anyone doubt him? He was not Jack the Ripper, he said, before refusing to talk about the Chandler case because of a confidentiality agreement, other than saying that he 'didn't want to go through a long, drawn-out affair with OJ.' On and on he went, making matters worse with every word he uttered, practically inviting that lawsuit, making himself seem even more distanced from the world, while Bashir lapped it all up.

It was an unmitigated disaster. The whole tenor of the piece was extremely hostile, with Bashir commenting darkly that Neverland was a 'dangerous' place for children. For Michael, this was all too much. 'Martin Bashir persuaded me to trust him that this would be an honest and fair portrayal of my life and told me he was "the man that turned Diana's life around,"' he said in a videotaped statement. 'Today I feel more betrayed than perhaps ever before – that someone, who had got to know my children, my staff and me, whom I let into my heart and told the truth, could then sacrifice the trust I placed in him and produce this terrible and unfair programme.'

This became more clear when Michael released some

filming of his own. 'Your relationship with your children is spectacular,' Bashir was pictured saying to Michael. 'It almost makes me weep when I see you with them because your interaction with them is so natural, so loving, so caring.'

There was other footage in the rebuttal video, too. Bashir had criticised Michael's decision to keep his children in masks when they were in public: apart from this being a perfectly sensible security precaution in the light of their father's fame, Debbie was filmed talking about the fact that it was her idea, not Michael's. She also addressed the subject of sharing beds head-on, pointing out that she shared a bed with visitors when she was watching TV. Bashir was then shown again, telling Michael that he thought it was wonderful that he allowed children to visit Neverland.

But that certainly wasn't the message that came across in the documentary, and so the damage was done. The original film, broadcast on 4 February 2003, was watched by 15 million in the UK and 38 million in the US; rather less saw the subsequent film that Michael put out. And there was widespread disquiet about a grown man sharing his bed with children. It had been foolish for Michael to admit to this, but what he had done, in effect, was to invite a lawsuit, with all the money that could potentially be at stake. That, of course, is exactly what happened next.

Michael was actually in the company of his long-term friend Mark Lester, Blanket's godfather, when he saw what Bashir had done. Mark described that time to the *Mail On Sunday*. 'We were together in Miami when he saw it,' he said. 'Michael was just dumbstruck. He didn't shout. I never heard him once raise his voice his whole life, but he was very upset. Most of all, he just seemed confused by it all.'

Mark, who had known Michael for years, was not alarmed by the scene in which he was shown putting his arm around Gavin and holding hands with him: he knew exactly what Michael was like. 'That was Michael,' he said. 'He didn't see a problem with it. He just loved children. He saw himself as the Pied Piper. At Neverland he had an enormous oil painting covering one wall and it was Michael as the Pied Piper, leading hundreds of children of all colours, races, sizes. Some were in wheelchairs. Michael was dancing and these kids were in a huge crocodile line behind him.

'He always told me he wrote his songs for the age group of 10 to 14. He would never do anything to hurt anyone and I don't believe that anything ever happened with Gavin Arvizo. When I thought about what Michael did for that family, it made me sick to think that they could do that to him. The experience did make him more withdrawn. He took himself away and hid from everyone.'

In the UK, accustomed to the rumbustious excesses of the tabloid press, the reaction of the public tended to be that Michael had been foolish and brought it on himself. However, in the US, there was a good deal more sympathy for Michael and some very understandable revulsion towards Martin Bashir. The *New York Times* wrote that Michael was, 'almost touching in his delusional naiveté: a victim of his own psyche and also of his interviewer's callous self-interest marked as sympathy.' Meanwhile, *USA Today* labelled the episode, 'unduly intrusive.'

After that, Michael's use of prescription drugs increased rapidly. Between 1996 and 2003, Dieter Wiesner was his manager and he described the state that his former client got himself into. 'It broke him, it killed him,' he revealed. 'He took a long time to die, but it started that night. Previously, the drugs were a crutch but after that they became a necessity. I'll never forget the day at Neverland when he walked into the kitchen to eat. He was off his face; he couldn't even bring the fork up to his mouth. There he was, one of the most talented guys on the planet, unable to even eat because he was so doped up.' And of course, after the trial, Michael would get even worse, but then there was no one around to help him.

Martin Bashir did very well out of the situation, landing a $1 million a year contract with ABC. After

Michael's death, perhaps upset at the controversy over the programme, he came out with the following. 'I think it's worth remembering that he was probably, singly, the greatest dancer and musician the world has ever seen,' he said. 'Certainly when I made the documentary, there was a small part of that which contained a controversy concerning his relationship with other young people. But the truth is that he was never convicted of any crime; I never saw any wrongdoing myself. And whilst his lifestyle may have been unorthodox, I don't believe it was criminal. And I think the world has now lost the greatest entertainer it's probably ever known.'

It is said by many people who knew him that as soon as they saw Michael admitting on TV that he shared his bed with children, that was it: his career was at an end. That proved to be the case, but it needn't have been so, were it not for his untimely death. The repercussions from the documentary and the subsequent trial sent Michael into exile, but it was not necessarily all over for him, not at all. When the first dates for the O2 extravaganza were announced, they sold out in hours. When the number of concerts soared to 50, all of those went quickly, too. Michael was still loved and revered by many, no matter how unwise his lifestyle choices, and as those few snatched shots of him performing in rehearsals showed, he never lost any of his talent, no matter what life threw at him.

CHAPTER TWELVE
THE FINAL YEARS

After the fiasco of Martin Bashir's documentary, it was inevitable that trouble would ensue, and so it did: on 18 December 2003, Michael was charged on 10 counts, including child molestation of Gavin Arvizo. It was a case many people believed should never have gone to court. For a start, the allegations referred to events that happened after the documentary was aired, not before, and it was remarked that given the outcry Michael's admission to sharing a bed with children had provoked, he was hardly likely to start abusing Arvizo now, if he hadn't done so previously. Arvizo denied, both publicly and privately, that any abuse had occurred, but Gavin's mother Janet had a history of attempting to claim money. Someone, somewhere, was determined to get Michael Jackson, however, and so the next year and a half of his life would be dominated by the proceedings.

It certainly seemed that he was receiving particularly brutal treatment because of who he was. When Michael first learned of the charges in November 2003, while he was recording in Las Vegas, he voluntarily returned to LA to give himself up for arrest, for which pains he was photographed in public, in handcuffs. Compared to US music producer Phil Spector, who was charged with murder and only required to post bail of $1 million (and was subsequently convicted of murdering actress Lana Clarkson after a five-month retrial), Michael's own bail was posted at $3 million. There were also some who saw racism in the way he was treated: there are plenty of African Americans who believe the justice system is skewed against them and while Michael might not have looked it anymore, he was still the most famous black man in the world.

The judge was Rodney S. Melville, and Michael had Thomas A. Mesereau Jr as his lawyer. His weight began to plummet as behind the scenes, he was becoming ever more heavily dependent on drugs. But still his family rallied round: Katherine, Joe and Jermaine were in court every day of the trial; other family members also publicly denied an impropriety.

It was at this stage that Michael became involved with the Nation of Islam (NOI), a controversial black activist group headed by the Honorable Minister Louis Farrakhan. Grace Rwaramba was now the children's nanny, and had links with Farrakhan: it was she who suggested that Michael hire some of the men to become bodyguards to the children. Ultimately, they became bodyguards for Michael as well, leading to fears that he had fallen under their influence and had even, like his brother Jermaine, converted to Islam. There has never been any proof that this was the case, but what most certainly was apparent was that in his hour of need, prominent members of the black community rose up to support their brother, whereas a lot of the show-business friends only too happy to claim him as one of their own after his death stayed well away during this crisis in his life. Elizabeth Taylor continued to support her friend, perhaps fuelled not just by her conviction of his innocence, but the fact that she didn't really care what anybody thought about her anymore. She knew exactly how gruelling it could be, to be at the top of your game and then fall from grace.

Another person who provided a great deal of moral support was Michael's defence lawyer, Tony Capozzola. He never talked about the trial while Michael was alive, but in the wake of his death revealed quite how frightened his former client had become.

'Michael was terrified that he might be convicted and go to jail – that was his worst fear,' he revealed. 'He called me many, many times after court; he called me late at night. He was very emotional and crying in a lot of the calls; it was a really tough time for him, he was unstable. Our relationship developed into a friendship and if I wasn't there, he spoke to my wife. Michael was frightened to be in custody: he knew that if he went to prison as a child molester, terrible things would have happened to him. He was scared he would be attacked and even molested by other prisoners. Physically, he was very frail and very frightened about that.'

Indeed, Michael became so overwrought that he actually considered suicide. 'He would constantly say, "Tony, do you think I'm going to jail? I need you to be honest with me,"' Capozzola revealed. 'He would break down, his voice would tremble and he'd be sobbing. He never said, "I'm going to kill myself," but he said, "I can't go to jail, I just can't." He implied that he would have to find another way out. I tried everything to keep his mind away from that, but I was worried he would do something stupid. In court, Michael was completely quiet, the perfect defendant. He wasn't arrogant, he didn't say a word – he just sat there, frightened. They said all these terrible things about him. Michael was upset, even sick.'

Even now, however, Michael didn't seem to understand why he had managed to land himself in so much trouble. 'He could not understand society's evil thoughts about him because of his mental set. He was Peter Pan, "Why do they think I'm evil?" he'd say,' Tony related. '"I don't know why everyone thinks I'm guilty." I had to be very blunt with him, I told him, "Because you're a 48-year-old man and you got interviewed by Martin Bashir and told him you sleep with children, that doesn't go on in America or in most civilised countries; a man does not sleep with children." Michael told me nothing sexual went on, and I believed him, but I said again that sleeping with kids doesn't go in today's society, but he told me, "That's society's problem and not mine." In other words, they are the dirty old men.'

By the end of the trial, Michael was an absolute wreck. 'The night before the jury went out, Michael hit an all-time low,' continued Tony. 'His voice was trembling and he said, "I'm very worried, I'm very worried." His biggest concern was his children. He said, "If I go to jail, I don't know what will happen to my family, who will look after them?" Michael Jackson was never an evil person, but he was certainly a target for those who are.'

Gavin Arvizo and his younger brother testified: their stories did not match up. Several other boys, who Michael was accused of molesting – Macaulay Culkin, Wade Robson and Brett Barnes – were also called to the trial and ended up taking the stand for the defence. All denied any wrongdoing on Michael's part.

Macaulay Culkin's time on the stand was particularly

instructive. A child star himself, he was now a young adult and his utter disdain for the proceedings highlighted the circus it had become. The exchange between Culkin and Thomas Mesereau went like this:

Mesereau: 'Did Mr. Jackson ever molest you?'
Culkin: 'Never.'
Mesereau: 'Did Mr. Jackson ever improperly touch you?'
Culkin: 'Absolutely not.'
Mesereau: 'Has Mr. Jackson ever touched you in any sexual type of way?'
Culkin: 'No.'

In fact, Macaulay went on to call the allegations 'absolutely ridiculous' before the prosecutor, Ron Zonen, suggested he could have been molested while he was asleep. 'I think I'd realise if something like that was happening to me,' said Culkin, rather coolly.

He then went on, rather wearily, to explain the basis of the friendship: the shared experience of child stardom: 'I was essentially a normal kid who happened to be an actor and the next thing I know, I'm just this thing, where people are hiding in the bushes and trying to take your picture. And people are trying to profit from you, or the next thing you know, you have a million acquaintances and no more friends anymore. It was like that and [Michael] understood that.'

The other two boys, Wade Robson and Brett Barnes, and their mothers also testified: all said the allegations were preposterous. Debbie Rowe was called by the prosecution: she said Michael was an excellent father and totally innocent of all charges. A psychiatrist testified Michael did not have the psychological profile of a paedophile – rather, he gave every indication of severely arrested development, giving him an emotional age of about 10.

Then there were the witnesses used by the prosecution. Several members of Jackson's household staff appeared in court, but under cross-examination were found to be unreliable witnesses.

As Michael's weight continued to drop, there were various dramas. At one point, he was hospitalised with flu-like symptoms and complained constantly of back pain. On another occasion, he was late and threatened with his bail being revoked; he turned up still clad in his pyjama bottoms, held up by aides without whom he would barely have been able to stand. 'He was ill and frightened, which made him look weirder,' said Tony Capozzola.

On 13 June 2005, Michael Jackson was found not guilty on all 10 charges. Though completely vindicated, the trial left him a broken man. He couldn't even take refuge in his beloved Neverland any more, because it had been violated by the trial. His inner world was laid bare, nothing private left untouched, and he felt utterly humiliated. Life really would never be the same again, and so began a rather nomadic existence that would last for several years.

Michael first went to live in Bahrain, about as far away from the prying eyes of the Western press as can be imagined; he was a guest of the Royal family, while Neverland itself was shut down. Given that his income was not what it once was, there were various stories about Neverland being sold: that was not, however, the case, and in 2006, Michael also struck a deal with Sony to refinance a loan he had taken out against their jointly-owned back catalogue. He and Sony went on to purchase Famous Music LLC, thus getting hold of the back catalogues of Eminem, Shakira and more: whatever the truth about the state of his finances, this package alone was estimated to bring him an income of about $75 million a year.

Although she testified in his favour at the trial, Debbie Rowe put in a bid for custody of the children in 2004: matters were settled with her, too. Michael appeared to have become more accepting of his life and everything that had happened within it: at an appearance with fans in Japan, during which he did not perform, he said, 'I've been in the entertainment industry since I was 6 years old. As Charles Dickens says, "It's been the best of times, the worst of times," but I would not change my career. While some have made deliberate attempts to hurt me, I take it in my stride because I have a loving family, a strong faith, and wonderful friends and fans who have, and continue, to support me.'

The nomadic life continued, with Michael spending time in France and a castle in Ireland. He was just about always with his children, always veiled in public, of course, and frequently extolled the joys of fatherhood. It was his main raison d'être, now.

'They mean, it's hard to put it into words because they mean everything,' he told talk-show host Geraldo Rivera. 'The way you would explain how your children make you feel... They're the world for me: I wake up and I'm ready for the day because of them. I get them breakfast, I change diapers; if they want to read, we do a lot of reading, we play hide and seek, we play blindfold and have a wonderful time with it.' At last Michael had children that he could play with without this causing comment, but their time together was to be cut short.

On 15 November 2006, Michael was presented with the Diamond Award at the World Music Awards for selling over 100 million albums. The following month, he attended the funeral of James Brown, the great star the young Michael watched and emulated as he began to learn to dance, aged 5. He paid a public tribute: 'James Brown is my greatest inspiration,' he said. 'When I saw him move, I was mesmerised. I never saw a performer move like James Brown. James Brown, I shall miss you, and I love you so much. Thank you for everything.'

Various anniversaries came and went. On the twenty-fifth anniversary of *Thriller*, *Thriller 25* was released, with a new song, 'For All Time', and re-mixes of several older ones. It got to No. 1 in eight countries and in 12 weeks sold 3 million copies worldwide. Michael still had that old magic: even if not on the scale of past glories, a new Michael Jackson album was still an event. Then, on his fiftieth birthday, Sony BMG released a series of compilation albums, with the tracks chosen by fans, taken from Michael's career, both as a solo artist and with his brothers in the Jackson 5.

Money remained an issue, however, and so it was that in 2008, plans were formulated for a huge comeback at London's O2 Arena, called This Is It. Initially, it was planned that Michael would perform in 10 concerts, but the demand for tickets was so huge that the run was expanded to 50 nights. It was a risk, given that Michael hadn't performed in public for years, but one that everyone involved was prepared to take. He certainly still had pulling power: 'By the end of the 50 concerts, 1 million fans will have witnessed one of the greatest musical events in history,' said the statement on the MichaelJacksonLive webpage. 'The figures speak for themselves – 360,000 tickets sold in 18 hours during the pre-sale so far, that is

20,000 tickets per hour, 33 tickets per minute!' Indeed, demand was so great, the Ticketmaster website began experiencing technical problems.

But those close to Michael were increasingly concerned that he just wasn't up to it. His last concert had been 12 years previously; privately, it was known his reliance on prescription drugs had now spiralled totally out of control. There were more concerns still when it was announced that the start date of the concerts had been pushed back: originally the run was to begin on 8 July 2009, but now this was pushed back to the 13th.

The concert promoters were keen to explain that nothing was wrong: it was only logistics that had forced the delay. At a press conference Randy Phillips, president and CEO of AEG Live, admitted that it was a 'tough' decision one to make, but a $20 million show had grown in size and complexity. There were no plans to change any more dates, although, 'if Michael were to get ill, that's possible.' However, Michael wasn't going to get ill. The changes had 'absolutely nothing to do with [Michael's] health.'

Kenny Ortega, who was working with Michael on the show, added the original plan, 'would have put us into the O2 one night before we opened to the world. It just wasn't practical for safety reasons and professional reasons.'

As for Michael's health – 'I would trade my body for

his tomorrow,' said Phillips. 'He's in fantastic shape. He's not dying of skin cancer.'

Ortega was also extremely positive. 'These choices [the delay] were made purely based on the practical needs and the responsible needs of putting up a first-class production,' he said. 'Physically and mentally, we're having a blast. We're having a great time. This is a high time for Michael, he's enjoying this. He's loving the creative process.' It would be, 'the concert of a lifetime. We have all been inspired to really raise the bar on our thinking.'

'It's going to cost us well north of $20 million dollars and it's incredible,' added Phillips. 'This is one hell of a show! It's going to be worth the wait.'

★ ★ ★

Michael Jackson's memorial service was held on 6 July 2009 at the Staples Center in Los Angeles, where he had been rehearsing for his forthcoming shows. His frail body lay in a £15,000 solid bronze coffin, plated with 14-carat gold and lined with blue velvet. It was placed at the front of the stage, covered with flowers and wreaths, while in the background a large screen read, 'In loving memory of Michael Jackson, King of Pop, 1958–2009.' The Jackson clan was out in force: his brothers and sisters lined the front row of the auditorium; the men of the family all dressed in black suits, yellow ties and, in honour of their brother's famous signature look, one white sequinned glove. Michael's children were there, and his parents. The family might have had their problems while Michael was among us, but they were certainly united in the wake of his death.

The world of celebrity was out in full, too. Elizabeth Taylor was not present, saying she couldn't take the hoopla, nor was Diana Ross. But everyone else was there: Larry King, Brooke Shields, Magic Johnson, the Kardashian sisters, Don King, Lou Ferrigno (Michael's former fitness trainer, aka the Incredible Hulk), Wesley Snipes, Spike Lee and Kobe Bryant of the Los Angeles Lakers, to name but a few.

There was a moment of silence at the beginning, followed by the organ strains of 'Soon and Very Soon'. Jackson family friend, Pastor Lucious Smith of the Friendship Baptist Church in Pasadena, got up to speak. 'First, and foremost, this man was our brother, our son, our father and our friend,' he said. 'In his very beautiful and very human heart, Michael Jackson wanted nothing more than to give love to the world. May this moment of remembrance bring comfort and healing to those who loved our friend.'

Matters kicked off with a message from Nelson Mandela, calling Michael a 'giant and a legend', while Mariah Carey sang the Jackson 5 hit, 'I'll Be There'. Then Queen Latifah took to the stage. 'Michael was the biggest star on earth,' she said. 'In Birmingham, Alabama, and in Birmingham, England, we are missing Michael Jackson: we are the world.' Lionel Richie sang 'Jesus Is Love', then Berry Gordy got up to speak, remembering the brilliant young boy he had met all those years ago. After the Motown 25 celebration and Michael's rendition of 'Billie Jean', 'Michael Jackson went into orbit and never came down.' Gordy then said that the title, King of Pop, just wouldn't do it anymore: 'He is simply the greatest entertainer who ever lived.' He received a standing ovation.

There was a great deal of footage of Michael from throughout his life, the very earliest days to the more recent triumphs. Put together like this, the full impact of what he had achieved was mesmerising, even to an audience who already knew his story and quite how much he had put into his life. This was a celebration, as well as a remembrance of one of show business's greatest stars.

Britain's representative up on stage was Shaheen Jafargholi, the 12-year-old star of *Britain's Got Talent*. Michael had seen his performance, singing the Jackson 5 hit, 'Who's Lovin' You', and was much taken with it, inviting the youngster to duet with him at the O2. Instead, Shaheen was singing at his memorial service, where he repeated the number to much acclaim and received a standing ovation for his powerful tribute. 'I love Michael Jackson,' he said. 'I just want to thank him so much for blessing me and every single individual on earth with his music.'

The Revd. Al Sharpton, a famed civil rights activist, delivered the eulogy in a fiery moment of bravado that summed up everything best about Michael's life: he 'broke down the colour curtain,' he said. He, 'brought whites and blacks and Latinos together.' He 'made it possible for Tiger Woods and even Barack Obama to succeed'. 'He outsang his cynics,' Sharpton continued. 'He outdanced his doubters; he outperformed the pessimists. Every time he got knocked down, he got back up. Every time you counted him out, he came back in. Michael never stopped. Michael never stopped. Michael never stopped. There wasn't nothing strange about your daddy,' he said, turning to Michael's children. 'It was strange what your daddy had to deal with!'

One famous name after another queued up to pay their respects and share memories, including Jennifer Hudson and Stevie Wonder. 'This is a moment that I wished that I didn't live to see come,' said Stevie, clearly very upset. 'But as much that I can say that I mean it, I do know that God is good and I do know that as much as we may feel – and we do – that we need Michael here with us, God must have needed him far more.'

Usher, Martin Luther King III and his sister Bernice all spoke. Magic Johnson made everyone laugh with an anecdote about Michael eating Kentucky Fried Chicken, while Brooke Shields did similarly when she recalled that on the eve of Elizabeth Taylor's wedding to Larry Fortensky, she and Michael broke into her room at Neverland because they couldn't wait until the following day to see the dress.

She was, however, clearly struggling to hold back the tears. 'Michael was one of a kind,' she said, talking about their bond. 'I used to tease him: "I started when I was 11 months old, you're a slacker! You were what? 5?" We never collaborated together: we never performed together or danced on the same stage, although he did try in vain one night, unsuccessfully, to teach me the Moonwalk... What we did do was laugh.'

Various Jacksons spoke. Jermaine thanked everyone for coming. Marlon said part of his brother, 'will live forever within me and within us all. How much pain and ridicule can one man take? Maybe now they'll leave you alone. You have finished your work here on earth and the Lord has called on you to come.' He asked Michael to give his late twin Brandon a hug and then burst into tears.

With a gospel choir supporting them, Michael's entire family then got up on stage and sang 'Heal The World'. However, the most touching moment of the service came towards the end. Michael's children had rarely been seen in public before and had never been heard to speak, but a clearly overcome Paris was determined to pay tribute. With Janet and LaToya at her side, Paris took up the microphone, in front of a global audience estimated at about one billion. 'Ever since I was born, Daddy has been the best father I could imagine,' she said, before the poor child burst into tears. 'I just want to say I love him so much.' Leaning against her Aunt Janet, she gave way to sobs.

Pastor Lucious Smith closed the ceremony: 'All around us are people of different cultures, different religions, different nationalities,' he said. 'And yet the music of Michael Jackson brings us together.'

★ ★ ★

Michael Jackson should be remembered for two things: his music and his children. Unquestionably one of the greatest performers of the twentieth century, he broke boundaries, created unforgettable pop and entertained billions. He had an extraordinary life full of extraordinary achievements. His name will live on long after all the smoke and mirrors that swirled around him for so much of his life has gone.

As for his children, they were devoted to him. That, ultimately, is what mattered to Michael more than anything else.

And so, farewell to the Peter Pan of Pop: like his fictional counterpart, he didn't want to grow old – and of course, Michael Jackson never did grow old. Michael Jackson, rest in peace.

THE COMPLETE MICHAEL JACKSON DISCOGRAPHY

STUDIO ALBUMS (WITH TRACK LISTS)
Got to Be There (1972 – Motown Records)
Songs:
'Ain't No Sunshine'
'Girl, Don't Take Your Love From Me'
'Got to Be There'
'In Our Small Way'
'I Wanna Be Where You Are'
'Love Is Here And You Are Gone'
'Maria (You Were The Only One)'
'Rockin' Robin'
'Wings of My Love'
'You've Got a Friend'

Ben (1972 – Motown Records)

Songs:

'Ben'

'Everybody's Somebody's Fool'

'Greatest Show on Earth'

'In Our Small Way'

'My Girl'

'People Make The World Go Round'

'Shoo-Be-Doo-Be-Doo-Da-Day'

'We've Got a Good Thing Going'

'What Goes Around Comes Around'

'You Can Cry on My Shoulder'

Music & Me (1973 – Motown Records)

Songs:

'With a Child's Heart'

'Up Again'

'All the Things You Are'

'Happy'

'Too Young'

'Doggin' Around'

'Johnny Raven'

'Euphoria'

'Morning Glow'

'Music and Me'

Forever, Michael (1975 – Motown Records)

Songs:

'We're Almost There'

'Take Me Back'
'One Day in Your Life'
'Cinderella Stay Awhile'
'We've Got Forever'
'Just a Little Bit of You'
'You Are There'
'Dapper Dan'
'Dear Michael'
'I'll Come Home to You'

Off the Wall (1979 – Epic Records)
Songs:
'Don't Stop 'Til You Get Enough'
'Rock With You'
'Working Day And Night'
'Get On the Floor'
'Off The Wall'
'Girlfriend'
'She's Out Of My Life'
'Burn This Disco Out'
'It's the Falling In Love'
'I Can't Help It'

Thriller (1982 – Epic Records)
Songs:
'Wanna Be Startin' Somethin''
'Baby Be Mine'
'The Girl Is Mine'
'Thriller'

'Beat It'
'Billie Jean'
'Human Nature'
'P.Y.T. (Pretty Young Thing)'
'The Lady in My Life'

Bad (1987 – Epic Records)
Songs:
'Bad'
'The Way You Make Me Feel'
'Speed Demon'
'Liberian Girl'
'Just Good Friends'
'Another Part of Me'
'Man in The Mirror'
'I Just Can't Stop Loving You'
'Dirty Diana'
'Smooth Criminal'
'Leave Me Alone'

Dangerous (1991 – Epic Records)
Songs:
'Jam'
'Why You Wanna Trip On Me'
'In The Closet'
'She Drives Me Wild'
'Remember the Time'
'Can't Let Her Get Away'
'Heal the World'

'Black or White'
'Who Is It'
'Give In To Me'
'Will You Be There'
'Keep the Faith'
'Gone Too Soon'
'Dangerous'

HIStory: Past, Present And Future: Book 1 (1995 – Epic Records)
Songs:
'Scream'
'They Don't Care About Us'
'Stranger in Moscow'
'This Time Around'
'Earth Song'
'D.S.'
'Money'
'Come Together'
'You Are Not Alone'
'Childhood'
'Tabloid Junkie'
'2 Bad'
'HIStory'
'Little Susie'
'Smile'

Invincible (2001 – Epic Records)

Songs:

'Unbreakable'

'Heartbreaker'

'Invincible'

'Break of Dawn'

'Heaven Can Wait'

'You Rock My World'

'Butterflies'

'Speechless'

'2000 Watts'

'You Are My Life'

'Don't Walk Away'

'Privacy'

'Cry'

'The Lost Children'

'Whatever Happens'

'Threatened'

COMPILATIONS

The Best of Michael Jackson (1975)

One Day in Your Life (1981)

18 Greatest Hits (1983)

9 Singles Pack (1983)

14 Greatest Hits (1984)

E.T. the Extra-Terrestrial (1984)

Love Songs (with Diana Ross) (1987)

Singles Souvenir Pack (1988)

Motown's Greatest Hits (1992)

THE COMPLETE MICHAEL JACKSON DISCOGRAPHY

Tour Souvenir Pack (1992)
The Best of Michael Jackson & The Jackson 5ive (1997)
The Very Best of Michael Jackson with The Jackson Five (1999)
20th Century Masters – The Millennium Collection: The Best of Michael Jackson (2000)
Greatest Hits: HIStory, Vol. 1 (2001)
Number Ones (2003)
Off the Wall/Thriller (box set) (2004)
Bad/Dangerous (box set) (2004)
Michael Jackson: The Ultimate Collection (2004)
The Essential Michael Jackson (2005)
King of Pop (2008)
Gold (2008)
Dangerous/Dangerous – The Short Films (2008)
50 Best Songs: The Motown Years (2008)
The Collection (2009)
The Hits (2009)

OTHER ALBUMS (REMIX, HYBRIDS, ETC.)
Farewell My Summer Love (1984)
The Michael Jackson Mix (1987)
Blood on the Dance Floor: HIStory in the Mix (1997)
Thriller 25 (2008)

LIVE ALBUM RECORDS
One Night in Japan (2009)

GREATEST HITS RECORDS

A Collection of Michael Jackson's Oldies (1972)

The Best of Michael Jackson (1975)

Motown Superstar Series, Vol. 7 (1980)

Superstar (1980)

One Day in Your Life (1981)

Michael Jackson & The Jackson 5 (1983)

Fliphits (1983)

18 Greatest Hits (1983)

9 Singles Pack (1983)

14 Greatest Hits (1984)

16 Greatest Hits (1984)

Ain't No Sunshine (1984)

The Great Love Songs of Michael Jackson (1984)

Anthology (1986)

Ben/Got to Be There (1986)

Looking Back to Yesterday (1986)

Love Songs (with Diana Ross) (1987)

The Michael Jackson Mix (1987)

The Original Soul of Michael Jackson (1987)

Singles Souvenir Pack (1988)

Todo Mi Amor Eres Tu (1990)

Motown Legends (1990)

Five Remixes of the Track 'Bad' (1991)

Remix Collection (1992)

4 CD Singles Box (1992)

Motown's Greatest Hits (1992)

Tour Souvenir Pack (1992)

Dangerous Remix (1993)

Rockin' Robin (1993)

Anthology: The Best of Michael Jackson (1995)

HIStory: Past, Present and Future, Book I (1995)

Michael Jackson Story (1996)

Master Series (1997)

The Best of Michael Jackson & The Jackson 5ive (1997)

12 Inch Mixes (1998)

Got to Be There/Forever, Michael (1999)

Big Boy (1999)

The Very Best of Michael Jackson with The Jackson Five (1999)

Early Classics (1999)

Bad/Thriller (2000)

Forever, Michael/Music & Me/Ben (2000)

20th Century Masters - The Millennium Collection: The Best of Michael Jackson (2000)

Universal Masters Collection (2001)

Greatest Hits: HIStory, Vol. 1 (2001)

Love Songs (2002)

Very Best of Michael Jackson (2002)

Number Ones (2003)

Bad/Dangerous (2004)

Off the Wall/Thriller (2004)

Michael Jackson: The Ultimate Collection (2004)

Essential Collection (2005)

Best 1200 (2005)

The Essential Michael Jackson (2005)

Blood on the Dance Floor: HIStory in the Mix/Invincible (2006)

Collector's Box (2005)

Visionary: The Video Singles (2006)
Colour Collection (2007)
The Silver Spectrum Collection (2007)
The Instrumental Hits of Michael Jackson (2007)
Silver Collection (2007)
'70s Pop (2007)
Off the Wall/Invincible (2008)
Worth It (2008)
Celebrating 25 Years of Thriller (2008)
King of Pop (2008)
Gold (2008)
50 Best Songs: The Motown Years (2008)
Classic: Masters Collection (2008)
Dangerous/Dangerous - The Short Films (2008)
The Masters Collection (2008)
Classic (2009)
Hello World: The Motown Solo Collection (2009)
The Collection (2009)
Michael Jackson: The Stripped Mixes (2009)
The Hits (2009)
The Very Best of Michael Jackson (2009)
The Document Unauthorized (2009)
Best Selection (2009)

THE JACKSON 5 DISCOGRAPHY
Released by Motown Records as The Jackson 5
Diana Ross Presents the Jackson 5 (1969)
ABC (1970)
Third Album (1970)

The Jackson 5 Christmas Album (1970)
Maybe Tomorrow (1971)
Goin' Back to Indiana (1971)
Lookin' Through the Windows (1972)
Skywriter (1973)
The Jackson 5 in Japan (1973)
G.I.T.: Get It Together (1973)
Dancing Machine (1974)
Moving Violation (1975)
Joyful Jukebox Music (1976)
Boogie (1979)
The Jacksons: An American Dream Soundtrack (1992)

RELEASED BY CBS RECORDS AS THE JACKSONS:
The Jacksons (1976)
Goin' Places (1977)
Destiny (1978)
Triumph (1980)
The Jacksons Live! (1981)
Victory (1984)
2300 Jackson Street (1989)

MICHAEL JACKSON'S US NUMBER ONES
'Ben' (1972) – 1 week
'Don't Stop 'Til You Get Enough' (1979) – 1 week
'Rock With You' (1980) – 4 weeks
'Billie Jean' (1983) – 7 weeks
'Beat It' (1983) – 3 weeks
'Say Say Say' (1983) – 6 weeks

'We Are The World' (1985) – 4 weeks
'Bad' (1986) – 2 weeks
'I Just Can't Stop Loving You' (1987) – 1 week
'The Way You Make Me Feel' (1987) – 1 week
'Man in the Mirror' (1988) – 2 weeks
'Dirty Diana' (1988) – 1 week
'Black or White' (1991) – 7 weeks
'You Are Not Alone' (1995) – 1 week

MICHAEL JACKSON'S UK NUMBER ONES

'One Day in Your Life' (1981) – 2 weeks
'Billie Jean' (1983) – 1 week
'I Just Can't Stop Loving You' (1987) – 2 weeks
'Black or White' (1991) – 2 weeks
'You Are Not Alone' (1995) – 2 weeks
'Earth Song' (1995) – 6 weeks
'Blood on the Dance Floor' (1997) – 1 week

MICHAEL JACKSON FILMOGRAPHY

The Wiz (1978) – as Scarecrow
Captain EO (1986) – as Captain EO
Moonwalker (1988) – as Michael Jackson
Ghosts (1997) – as Maestro/Mayor/Ghoul/Skeleton
Men in Black II (2002) – as Agent M
Miss Cast Away (2004) – as Agent M